I am not a woman.

I am not a man.

I am not a person.

I am not myself.

I am a teacher.

May we each be an instrument of peace.

Sat Nam

ILana Fintz (Dharma Atma Kaur)

CONTENTS

The attitude of gratitude is the highest way of living, and is the biggest truth, the highest truth.

KUNDALINI YOGA

In this practice, you will go through stages as you adjust to the effects of the postures. In Kundalini Yoga, the emphasis is not on perfecting the physical posture, but on the experience and effects of it. Kundalini Yoga is for everyone regardless of any physical limitations

Your entire body can be seen as a geometric grid which uses the angles and triangles of the asanas. The body is fuelled by the breath or Prana and the mind is re-tuned by the repetition of mantra. Add concentrated eye-focus and body locks and you are physically different by the end of each kriya. These changes assist the physical and mental preparation of a meditative internal space.

"Kundalini Yoga is a science which works on the seven chakras, the arc line and the aura (the Eighth Chakra). It works directly on the total energy, and that flow of energy has one simple way: either you sway it or it sways you. Either you are above the energy and ride it, or you go below the energy and it rides you. That is where Kundalini Yoga fits in: you will learn to ride your energy, to experience it and penetrate any given situation to attain a balance.

What is Kundalini, actually? It is your creative potential. You experience it when the energy of the glandular system combines with the energy of the nervous system to create such a sensitivity that the totality of the brain receives signals and integrates them. Then you become totally and wholly aware, and your creative potential becomes available to you.

The Power of Kundalini Yoga lies in the actual experience. It goes right into your heart and extends your consciousness so you may have a wider horizon of grace and of knowing the truth. Ultimately you come to understand your existence in relationship to the universe and understand who you already are, and this brings you to the practical experience of Infinity. You can then radiate creativity and Infinity in all aspects of your daily life."

Yogi Bhajan

GO WITHIN OR GO WITHOUT.

WELCOME TO THE AQUARIAN AGE – THE AGE OF AWAKENING

WHAT IS THE AQUARIAN AGE?

From November 1991, we started the final shift between the Piscean age – an age dominated by machines and hierarchies – to the current Aquarian Age – an age ruled by awareness – information and energy.

5 KEY CHALLENGES IN THE AQUARIAN AGE:

1. Learning is not enough. We need to learn how to learn.

2. The age of paradox: More GLOBAL and more INDIVIDUAL at the same time. How do we balance these?

3. Nothing happens in isolation. We need to understand that, just as our minds, body and spirit are interconnected so are we as beings that share this planet. This means that every action has an impact, whether ecologically, economically or globally. Actions need to be mindful and measured.

4. Complexity is increasing. So too our need to find a sustainable system to deal with it.

5. In this age of more (information, technology, contact, choices, complexity), the human nervous system is being put under enormous pressure, giving rise to fatigue-related illnesses, depression and psychological and spiritual ailments that need to be identified, addressed and supported.

PISCEAN AGE:	AQUARIAN AGE
Motto: To be or not to be, that is the question of this "information age".	Motto: Be to be, that is the answer of this "integration age".
Information was controlled and hidden. Our goal was to learn, grow and become something.	Information is available. Finding it is not the main goal. Embodying it and living it through our words and actions becomes of primary importance.
Intentions and actions were hidden under masks we presented to the world.	Everything becomes revealed. The masks will come off and the unknown will become known.
Intellect and knowledge are everything when you want to become "something".	Intellect and knowledge cannot help us "be". Intuition, emotion and instinct need to be integrated to help us be wise, contained and complete.
Knowledge has an end goal in mind.	Change and learning is a lifelong pursuit.
Seek "outer" education and external knowledge and expertise.	Seek internal understanding and education in wisdom, self control, intuition and the use of the neutral mind.

Note to Teachers:
YOUR ROLE AS AN AQUARIAN TEACHER IN THE AQUARIAN AGE:

People are overwhelmed. Nervous systems are under pressure. They don't need more choice, they need the capacity to make better choices. The only way to counter balance this externally-driven over-stimulation is through its opposite – internally driven under-standing. This is where you come in, as guides to this inner world, you need to help students tap into their inner support tools that are present but dormant – instinct, intuition and innate wisdom. More than ever, we need this holy trinity to help us cut through the information and see past the masks to make better choices for ourselves, our communities and our planet.

THE FIVE SUTRAS OF THE AQUARIAN AGE

Yogi Bhajan gave us five Yogic Sutras that sum up the teachings for the Age of Aquarius. A sutra is a 'knot.' It's a complex spiritual concept reduced to one sentence. The knot can be untied and expanded upon by a spiritual teacher. Sutras allow sacred teachings to be protected by appearing harmless and are brief enough to be easily remembered by students in ancient times.

RECOGNIZE THAT THE OTHER PERSON IS YOU.

Apply this sutra in your own life and discover that what you praise in others is in fact a mirror of yourself which may not be revealed. You will also recognise that what you don't like in others is a denied part of yourself.

WHEN THE TIME IS ON YOU, START, AND THE PRESSURE WILL BE OFF.

This sutra is a reminder to start TODAY. Procrastination creates pressure. Once you have taken the first step, even if it is just one small thing, you will immediately feel a big release and gain the momentum to keep moving and growing.

VIBRATE THE COSMOS; THE COSMOS SHALL CLEAR THE PATH.

The Universe is a vibration of energy. We are either vibrating in harmony or disharmony with the Universe. What we put out we receive back. To vibrate with the Universe is to vibrate the higher frequencies of love, compassion and kindness thus attracting loving support and divine direction.

THERE IS A WAY THROUGH EVERY BLOCK.

Use this sutra to recognize that the challenges you face today are opportunities for growth. Life challenges help us build our spiritual muscles to grow and expand on our soul's journey. As with any muscle-building, it's often a difficult journey to get the desired results.

UNDERSTAND THROUGH COMPASSION OR YOU WILL MISUNDERSTAND THE TIMES.

Compassion lives in the heart. When we are judgmental and turn away from suffering we are misunderstanding the times. Apply this sutra to any difficult situation and realise that we are all in it together. We are all one. It will help you forgive and resolve.

One powerful way to get into alignment and to truly embody these Sutras is through a regular practice of Kundalini Yoga, meditation and chanting sacred sounds.

IN THE BEGINNING

THE ADI MANTRA - THE PRIMAL MANTRA

Bring your hands into prayer mudra. Inhale deeply and chant the Adi Mantra in one exhalation. Chant this mantra 3 times.

Ong Namo
Guru Dev Namo

Create a nasal sound as you chant ONG. Vibrate the sound up through the centre of your head. This helps to stimulate the third eye and awaken our neutral mind.

ONG is the creative (female and flowing). NAMO means I bow. GURU DEV is the divine wisdom or teacher (masculine and stable). NAMO we align with it.
We are tuning into our higher selves to become more aware of the divine space within.
This mantra is used for "tuning in" to the vibration of self-knowledge linking us to the teachings of Yogi Bhajan and the Golden Chain of teachers which helps to connect and guide us through the practice.

THE MANGALA CHARAN - FOR PROTECTION

After Adi Mantra you can chant the Mangala Charan.
A mantra for protective power. As you chant the mantra feel the sound vibration encircling the space you are in.
Chant this mantra 3 times.

Aad Guray Nameh
Jugaad Guray Nameh
Sat Guray Nameh
Siri Guru Dayvay Nameh

I bow to the primal teacher
I bow to the truth throughout the ages
I bow to the true wisdom
I bow to the great unseen wisdom

NAMEH is 'I bow' to what is present, to what is past and what will always be forever into the future and connect with what is unseen.
With these 2 mantras we set an intention to connect to the significant forces of grounding, (stillness – male) and flowing, (movement – female). Finding freedom and inner peace to live in the universal flow of oneness.

THE BIJ MANTRA - THE SEED MANTRA

A Bij is a seed containing all the knowledge of the tree.

Sat Nam

It is translated as "Truth is my Identity" As I stand in my truth, I embody my truth, I flow in my truth. When we chant SAT NAM we are planting a seed of truth into our consciousness. It is a sound that contains all the elements SA TA NA MA, holding the vibration that connects us to our true essence. One of the important components of yoga is how it affects your mental state in your life. How are you showing up for yourself and your relationship with yourself and your higher infinite self - this is also called GOD.

This mantra can be used mentally throughout the kriya - inhale SAT and exhale NAM.
It is also the final sound vibration chanted at the end of the class. Sat is chanted 8 x longer than Nam.

May the long time sun shine upon you,
all love surround you,
and the pure light within you,
guide your way on.

STAY FOCUSED

Drishti is a Sanskrit word meaning "sight" and refers to the gazing technique practiced while holding a yoga pose. Directing the gaze physically impacts the optic nerve as it travels from the eyes to the centre of the brain. Various eye positions cause the optic nerve to apply variable pressures to major glands and gray matter. More than just reducing external distractions, the eye-focus is a powerful meditation technique.

THIRD EYE POINT: Closed eyes are gently raised to the Brow Point, at the centre of the forehead a little above the eyebrows. This part of the forehead corresponds to the sixth chakra and stimulates the pituitary gland and sushumna (central nerve channel of the spine).

TIP OF THE NOSE: Eyes are slightly crossed, looking along the nose to the top of its tip. Balances the ida, pingala, and sushumna (left, right and central nerve channels of the spine). Gazing at the tip of the nose stimulates the pineal gland and frontal lobe of the brain; controls the mind.

TIP OF THE CHIN: Closed eyes are rolled downwards to the centre of the chin. This location corresponds to the Moon Centre, a seat of emotions. Helps us to feel calm and centred.

TOP OF THE HEAD: Closed eyes roll upwards, as if looking through the very top, centre of the head. The Crown Chakra, stimulates the pineal gland. Gives the feeling of universal oneness.

1/10TH OPEN: Eyelids are light and relaxed, leaving a small opening between them. Shines light into the subconscious mind. Helps us to be calm, present, develop intuition and feel our feelings.

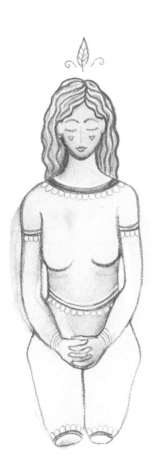

KEEP UP WITH THE TIMES

3 minutes energy flow start to open. Circulation and blood chemistry is affected. Meridians and nadis are activated and our cells are infused with fresh oxygen.

11 minutes the pituitary gland and the nerves start to learn and change. We begin to feel the vastness of Self.

22 minutes our three minds (negative, positive, and neutral) start to work together so our mental integration changes. Our highest potential can emerge.

31 minutes affects our whole mind and aura, and the tattwas are balanced. Our internal rhythms harmonize.
Our glands secrete optimally.

62 minutes the "shadow mind" and positive projection are integrated. The gray matter of the brain as well as the frontal lobe and pituitary, hypothalamus and pineal are stimulated. When this happens we can penetrate beyond our physical body, emotions and mental conditioning.

2 ½ hours completes the cycle of prana and apana so what we gain will hold through the cycle of the day. It holds change in the subconscious. Everything about us will be brighter and elevated.

40 days holds both a mystical and practical significance to transformation in our life and in many cultures.

In physiology, our skin cells on average take 40 days to renew, our red blood cells start dying from 40 days onwards and sperm count can be increased in 40 days.

Practice a particular kriya or mantra every single day for the same amount of time for **40 days.** This breaks negative habits that block you from expanding. New Moon is a good time to begin a meditation as it is easier to sustain your commitment.

90 days consecutively will establish a new habit in your conscious and subconscious minds based on the effect of the kriya or mantra. It will change you in a very deep way.

120 days will confirm the new habit of consciousness created by the kriya or mantra. The positive benefits of the kriya get integrated permanently into your psyche.

1000 days will allow you to master the new habit of consciousness that the kriya or mantra has promised. No matter what the challenge, you can call on this new habit to serve you.

The days we feel resistance are the days when we are clearing the most stuff!

EGO ERADICATOR

The more we identify with our ego, the more judgmental we will be toward others and the more we will project our own personality traits onto others. Ego Eradicator helps you move through the blocks and put stresses aside to have an elevated experience.

Ego Eradicator helps us to quickly find our centre by combining Breath of Fire with a specific arm position. In yogic theory, the thumbs are represented the ego. By pointing them up to the heavens we are setting an intention to go beyond the thoughts of the ego to access our higher selves.

How to do it:
Sit tall in Easy Pose. Press your fingertips firmly against the pads of your hands. Make sure they are tightly pressed down to generate and feel the energy moving. Give a double thumbs ups, and stretch them actively away from the fingers. Engage your arms firmly and draw them up to 60°, like a 'V' for victory. Visualise you are a funnel and decide what to bring into your experience. Focus your eyes at the brow point. Begin Breath of Fire. In your mind and heart be willing to look at your stuff, but at the same time be non-judgemental. Let go and allow.

To End:
Inhale deeply and hold the breath. With the breath held, draw the thumbs together overhead. When they meet, stretch the fingers. Exhale, let the arms slowly float down through your aura. Sit still for a moment to enjoy the energy and sensations from within!

Benefits:
With this arm position energetically, the posture is a heart and lung opener. Strengthens the navel chakra, thereby increasing vital energy. Repairs the balance between the sympathetic and parasympathetic nervous systems. This is a meditation to lean on when you need to shift, include it in your daily practice for **1-3 minutes.**

ONE BREATH AT A TIME

Prana is the body's vital or psychic energy, and yama means to control or master it. The basic effect of Pranayama is to channel and direct the flow of prana to alter physical and conscious states. The way we breathe, our rhythm and speed, has a direct influence on the nervous system, and vice versa.

Generally in life, we react automatically to experiences around us. When we do breathing exercises or meditate regularly, these automatic reactions and habits in the nervous system are reduced. Kundalini Yoga employs a wide range of breathing techniques which we can use for healing and clarity. It helps us reconnect with our subtler realms and instils a greater sense of purpose in life.

Conscious breathing is a process of becoming whole. Your body can only create x amount of energy and you have to distribute that energy throughout that day. Yogi Bhajan suggests that within every 31 minutes you must take at least 3 x conscious breaths.

The main breaths you will find in Kundalini Yoga:

LONG DEEP BREATHING - LDB

Inhale slowly. Divide torso into 3 regions. Consecutively fill each area: lower, mid and upper with the inhale. Exhale and reverse top to bottom using abdominal muscles

Benefits: Massages inner organs. Oxygenates blood stream. Stimulates pituitary and pineal glands. Good for digestion and freeing trapped energy. LDB is a tonic for calming the body and soothing the mind.

BREATH OF FIRE (BoF):

Actively pull and release the navel point and the solar plexus in and up. Start with 1 breath per second. Increasing to 2-3 breaths. Make sure that when you pull in your navel you are exhaling.

Benefits: Detoxifies and purifies the blood. Flushes pollutants from the lungs. Alkalises blood, giving instant energy. Stimulates the hypothalamus and pituitary which aids in muscle tone, vitality and physical endurance.

Boosts the benefits of a yoga pose. Infuses our nerves with new energy making our reflexes faster and brighter. Polishes our magnetic field making us feel more radiant.

Caution: Practice LDB if you are menstruating or pregnant.

LEFT NOSTRIL BREATHING

Block right nostril with right thumb.
Inhale, exhale through the left nostril only.

Benefits: Associated with lunar energy (ida nadi) calming, cooling, relaxing. Activates qualities of patience and letting go.
* Soothing to do any time you wish to relax or before sleep.

RIGHT NOSTRIL BREATHING

Block left nostril with left thumb. Inhale, exhale slow and deep through the right nostril only.

Benefits: Associated with solar energy (pingala nadi). Alleviates unbalanced mental and emotional states. Activates qualities of strong will, perseverance, motivation and the ability to take action and keep up!
* Quick energy boost: do Breath of Fire through the right nostril.

ALTERNATE NOSTRIL BREATHING:

Close right nostril using the right thumb. Inhale through the left nostril. Close the left nostril with ring finger. Release the thumb to exhale. Inhale through the right nostril, then close the right nostril and open the left nostril to exhale.

Benefits: Actively switching nostrils engages both hemispheres of the brain. Revitalises nervous system. Stimulates glandular system. Good for meditation prep or mood changer.
* Hold the left hand in gyan mudra

Caution: Don't practice this pranayama if you are experiencing sinus headaches, nasal congestion or other sinus related issues.

FOUR PART BREATH, SQUARE BREATHING

Exhale completely.
Inhale for a count of 4.
Hold in for a count of 4.
Exhale for 4.
Hold out for a count of 4.
In good time the count can be increased. Keep all counts equal.

Benefits: Affects sympathetic and parasympathetic nervous systems. Controls passion, pride and anger. Directs attention away from the external world.

WHISTLE BREATH:

Done on an inhale, exhale, or both. The whistle should be high-pitched. Focus the ears on the sound of the whistle.

Benefits: The gentle sound vibration of the whistle affects consciousness and glandular system. The movement of the lips stimulates the vagus nerve, regulating the heart beat. Controls muscle movement and contracts the muscles of the stomach and digestive tract.

CANNON BREATH:

Cannon Breath is Breath of Fire done through the 'O' shaped mouth - tongue is relaxed & the cheeks do not bulge.

Benefits: Cleanses the lungs, strengthens the parasympathetic nerves and stimulates the digestion.

*When exercises end with a powerful Cannon Breath exhale, imagine it as a powerful expulsion of anything that no longer serves your being.

SEGMENTED BREATH:

4 parts in : 1 part out: Heals, energises, uplifts
4 parts in : 4 parts out: Clarity, alertness, stimulates glands
8 parts in : 8 parts out: Calms, centres
8 parts in : 4 parts out: Focusing, energising
4 parts in : 8 parts out: Calms, unblocks, releases

*The ratios used are clearly defined and create stable, predictable, final states of mind and energy. Do not experiment.

Benefits: Harmonises our internal rhythms. Stimulates the central brain, nervous and glandular systems in different ways. Trains us to utilise our full lung capacity.

UJJAYI BREATH:

Inhale through your nose creating a constriction in the throat. Keep jaw, throat and neck relaxed. Feel the breath at the back of your throat. The audibility of the breath is compared to the sound of waves. Smooth and steady, continuous uninterrupted cycles of inhales and exhales. Within each cycle you spend the entire inhale filling up and entire exhale releasing breath. At no point do you hold the breath. Keep it seamless and smooth.

Benefits: Calming. Grounding. Works on the nervous system. Increases blood oxygenation and enhances lung capacity.

SITALI PRANAYAM:

Curl your tongue like a straw or pucker your lips.
Slightly extend tongue beyond your lips.
Inhale slowly through mouth. Exhale nostrils.

Benefits: Kidneys and adrenals. Reduces fevers, aids digestion, cleanses spleen and liver. Cools, calms body and mind.

BREATH RETENTION:

At the end of almost every posture the breath is suspended in or out. On the **Inhale**, push the lower abdomen out, then the middle abdomen, and finally the chest. Hold the breath, bring the chin in without creating tension in the neck or shoulders.

On the **Exhale,** release the air in the chest first, then the middle abdomen, and finally the lower abdomen. Hold the breath out, lift the chest, pull the chin in and relax.

Benefits: With habitual repetition the nervous system is reconditioned and repaired. Suspending the breath gives the muscles of the diaphragm, ribs and abdomen a break from the constant motion of the breath. This will support deep internal self transformation and healing.

Suspending the breath in can temporarily raise blood pressure and impact the sympathetic nervous system. Suspending the breath out lowers the blood pressure, relaxes circulation and impacts the parasympathetic nervous system.

On the suspended breath you can experience "Shuniya" or a "zero point". This is where the mind becomes still and you become the observer.

Caution: If you begin to feel dizzy, stop. You must build this practice with patience, awareness and inner quietness. Pushing past your capacity creates disharmony.

*Holding the breath in is harder than keeping it out, making breathing correctly a challenge. The reason for this is because the brain reacts when the CO_2 levels are too high, but not when the levels of O_2 fluctuate.

You are alive because of the breath of life. Use the breath of life in a slow potency to heal you, your mind, and to brighten your soul. Breathe in slowly, consciously, hold it consciously, and let it go consciously and slowly. Get to that rhythm, control it yourself. It can heal all, because it's the breath of life, which is the spirit in you, which is the soul in you, which is actually you, alive. ~ Yogi Bhajan

Inhale, and god approaches you. Hold the inhalation, and god remains with you. Exhale, and you approach god. Hold the exhalation, and surrender to god.
~ Krishnamacharya

MUDRA SEAL OF ENERGY

Our hands are an energy map of our consciousness and health. Each area of the hand corresponds to a certain area of the body or brain and to different emotions or behaviours. The various position of our hands is called a mudra and is a technique for giving clear messages to the mind-body energy system. By bringing our fingers and thumbs into certain positions we activate an energy flow through our 'nadi' system, as well as drawing from the elements and planets that each represents in the physical form.

GYAN MUDRA: Seal of Knowledge. Relates to expansion, wisdom and higher consciousness. Instils calmness and receptivity. Empowers the mind, nervous and endocrine system. Index finger symbolized by Jupiter and the Air (Vayu) element. The thumb, the ego carries energy of subconscious.

SHUNI MUDRA: Seal of Patience. Represents emotions. Encourages purity, discernment, commitment, compassion, and understanding. It helps turn negative emotions into positive ones. Middle finger is related to Saturn, Ether (Akash) element. Carries the energy of stability and strength.

SURYA MUDRA: Seal of Life
Gives us vitality and aliveness. It represents balance, energy, endurance, health and vitality. It can aid in positive change.
Speeds up metabolism and stimulates digestion. Ring finger is related to the Sun and the element of Earth (Pritvhi), resonates with the energy of the Solar Plexus and governs personal power.

BUDDHI MUDRA: Seal of Mental Clarity. Creates capacity for clear and open communication. Stimulates psychic development. Little finger is related to Mercury and the Water element. Resonates with our worldly and intellectual activities.

*Active Mudra. Bend the finger under the thumb so the fingernail presses against the fleshy thumb tip. Imparts active output as opposed to receptive.

PRANA MUDRA:
Activates the dormant energy within the body. This mudra symbolizes the vital energy of prana and will encourage the flow of this energy, making you feel energized and strong.

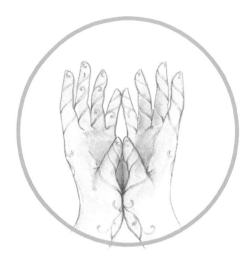

LOTUS MUDRA:
Balances the 5 tattvas of the conscious and subconscious mind.
Encourages feelings of being rooted, connected and strong like a lotus flower, while opening your heart to the joys of life.

BEAR GRIP:
Left palm faces out from body with thumb down, and right palm faces body, thumb up, and fingers are curled and hooked together. Stimulates the heart and intensifies concentration.

VENUS LOCK:
For sun energy, place the left thumb in the webbing between the thumb and index finger of the right hand. For moon energy, reverse to right thumb in the webbing. Channels sexual energy and ability to concentrate easily.
The mounds at the base of the thumbs represent Venus; sensuality and sexuality.

Shine the light of awareness into the darkest corners of your body.

WARM-UPS

In Kundalini Yoga, these postures are recognised as warms-ups to prepare our body to be as open and receptive as possible for the kriya

EASY POSE - SUKASANA:
Cross the legs comfortably at the ankles or both feet on the floor, pressing the lower spine forward to keep the back straight.

LOTUS - PADMASANA:
Lift left foot onto upper right thigh, then place right foot on left thigh as close to the body as possible. Enhances deep meditation.

ROCK POSE - VAJRASANA:
Sit on heels so that they press the nerves in the center of the buttocks. Knees and feet together. Facilitates digestion.

CELIBATE POSE - VIRASANA:
Stand on knees. Split the belly of calves and sit in between your heels. Toes pointing straight back. Press feet and shins down.

SHOULDER SHRUGS:
Inhale raise your left shoulder straight up toward your ear. Exhale down. Repeat second side. Keep your back straight and your chest upright.

BOAT POSE:
Lean back and balance on your sitting bones. Stretch arms parallel and legs to 60°. Lift heart. Focus on feeling empowered.

LIFE NERVE STRETCH:
Place right foot in the inseam of the left thigh. Hold onto big toe, ankle or thigh. Inhale up. Exhale down.

KUNDALINI LOTUS:
Peace fingers hold big toes. Press thumbs onto big toe nail. Balance on sacrum. Stretch the legs out to 60°. Straighten spine, legs and lift your heart.

CROW SQUAT:
Squat down knees pointing in the same direction as feet. Heels flat on ground. Back vertical to ground. Apply neck lock.

STANDING SIDE BEND:
Standing feet together. Arms up overhead in Prayer Mudra. Arch trunk toward the right. 1 minute each side.

STAFF POSE:
Sit with your legs extended together in front of torso. Firm thighs. Press downward. Move inner groins toward the sacrum. Flex your ankles. Press out through the heels.

TABLE TOP:
From staff pose bend knees. Feet parallel. Fingers pointed to feet. Lift hips up. Apply neck lock. Pressurizes thyroid and balances hips.

SPINAL FLEX, CAMEL RIDE:

Rock or Easy pose. Hands interlaced behind your head or holding onto your shins. Inhale forward, lift the chest up toward the chin. Exhale round the lower back. Keep head steady.

ROCK FORWARD BENDS:

Rock Pose. The movement is done to 10 beats:
Down on 1, up 2, down 3, up 4, down 5, up 6, down 7, up 8. Stay up for beats 9 and 10. Interlace fingers behind your neck. Also be done with fingers interlaced behind the lower back and arms stretch up when the forehead touches the ground.

WIDE LEG STRETCH POSE:

Both legs wide apart. Peace fingers hold onto big toes. Inhale centre. Exhale down to left/right knee. 1-3 minutes Helpful with elimination and feeling grounded.

VARIATION:

Keep legs wide apart. Inhale root down through the sit bones and stretch spine up. Exhale fold forward from the navel. Lead with heart. Head last to come down. 1-3 minutes. Opens up the pelvis and stretches the leg muscles.

WAKE UP SEQUENCE:

Inhale and exhale deeply. Move fingers and toes, rotate wrists and ankles in both directions.

Stretch the spine. Arms overhead, and do a few cat stretches to each side.

Rub the soles of the feet and the palms of the hands together.

Rock back and forth along the spine 5 to 10 times.
Follow this sequence at the end of savasana.

WARM-UP SEQUENCES:

Below is a variety of short warm-up sets for flexibility, grounding and strength.

Prepares the body and mind to be as open and receptive as possible for the kriya or meditation of your choice.

SERABANDANDA KRIYA TO HEAL: Exhale as you move from one to next asana.

Repeat cycle: 6-26 times with 2-10 min relaxation. Repeat cycle 3 times. Works with: valves between veins and arteries, circulation of blood and rejuvenation of the cells. Given by Yogi Bhajan for courage, stamina and fearless determination.

EXHALE:
Downward facing dog.
INHALE.

EXHALE: Downward facing
dog heels up. INHALE.
EXHALE: heels down.
INHALE.

EXHALE: Chin and chest
toward the ground,
buttocks up. INHALE.

EXHALE:
Upward facing dog.
INHALE.

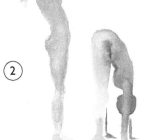

"Bend the negativity out of the human being."

1. MIRACLE BEND:
Heels together. Feet turned
out slightly. Lean back 20°.
LDB 2 mins. Fold forward.
Inhale pump navel. Exhale
pump on held exhale. 2 mins.

2. CRESCENT MOON:
Feet together.
Engage thighs and navel.
Lean to the left.
Long Deep Breath.
1 min each side.

3. DANCERS VARIATION:
Cow pose.
Right hand holding left foot.
LDB. 2 mins each side.
4. YOGA MUDRA
1 minute.

5. TREE POSE:
Hands in prayer above
the head or at the heart.
3-11 minutes each side.
Hold with LDB.

1. PIGEON PREP:
Left knee to left wrist. Left
foot toward right wrist.
Lengthen spine. 1-3 minutes
each side LDB. Stretches
quadricep muscles. Loosens
hips. Works on stomach and
liver meridians

2. BRIDGE POSE:
On back with feet flat.
Bend knees. Inhale lift hips up.
Apply light root lock.
BoF 1-3 minutes. Opens
circulation to the extremities.
Aids in liver's function to
purify the blood.

3. STAFF EXTENSION:
Extend legs forward. Arms
parallel to floor. Palm inward.
Thumbs up. Feet Flexed.
Inhale lengthen spine upward.
Exhale stretch forward 60°.

Light neck lock. 1-3 minutes
at a moderate pace. Works
on the adrenals, kidneys,
lungs and sciatic nerve.
Our thumbs connect to our
lung meridians.

(4)

1. SPINAL TWISTS:
Easy/Rock pose. Hands on shoulders, fingers in front, thumbs behind. arms parallel to floor. Inhale twist left. Exhale right. Rotate from the navel. Opens the lungs and ribcage region.

2. YOGA MUDRA:
Baby Pose, with the forehead on ground. Interlace fingers behind the lower back Brings energy to the head and the brain. Enhances relaxation and concentration.

3. CHAIR POSE:
Feet shoulder width apart. Bring thighs parallel to ground. Arms through inside legs. Hands on top of feet. Back straight. Strengthens your Nervous System and your potency.

4. MOUNTAIN POSE:
Standing feet hip width apart. Thighs back and apart. Tailbone forward. Root down through the four corners of your feet. Increase your strength and power, in feet, legs, and hips.

5. WINDMILL:
Standing with feet 60-90 cm apart. Arms parallel to ground. Palms facing forward. Inhale turn right. Exhale fold down touching left hand to/toward right foot. Repeat on left side. Stretches sciatic nerve and stimulates solar plexus.

6. CAT COW LEG EXTENSION:
Inhale, stretch left leg back and up. Exhale bring brow to knee. Switch sides. Keep abdominal muscles firm throughout. Slowly increase pace. Adjusts navel point. Balances Prana and Apana - Expansion and Elimination.

(5)

1. SUFI GRIND:
Easy pose. Hands on knees. Move abdominal area in small circles. Create heat in lower spine 26 x each direction. Tones inner organs stimulates heat at navel and warms up lower back.

2. NECK ROLL:
Chin to collarbone. Slowly and gently roll head in a circle 11 x each direction. Warms up small vertebrae in neck. Helps thyroid and parathyroid. Improves memory. Feel rooted in the heart centre.

3. CAT / COW:
On hands and knees. Hands shoulder width apart. Knees under hips. Inhale lift your head and lower the belly (cow). Exhale, chin to chest. Round your spine (cat). Continue with a smooth pace.

Increases flexibility of the neck, shoulders, and spine. Stretches the muscles of the hips, back, abdomen, chest, and lungs. Increases coordination. Massages and stimulates organs in the belly like the kidneys and adrenal glands.

Practicing a kriya initiates a sequence of physical and mental changes that simultaneously affect your body, mind, and soul.

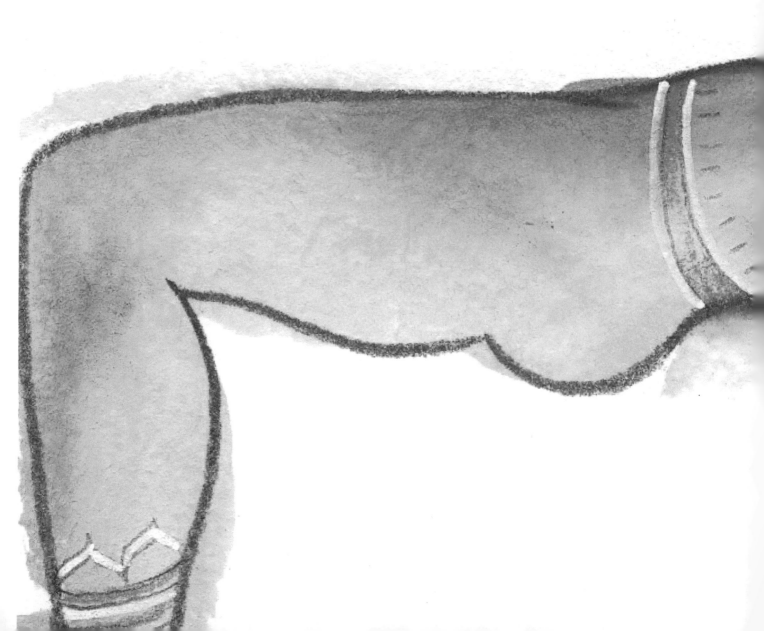

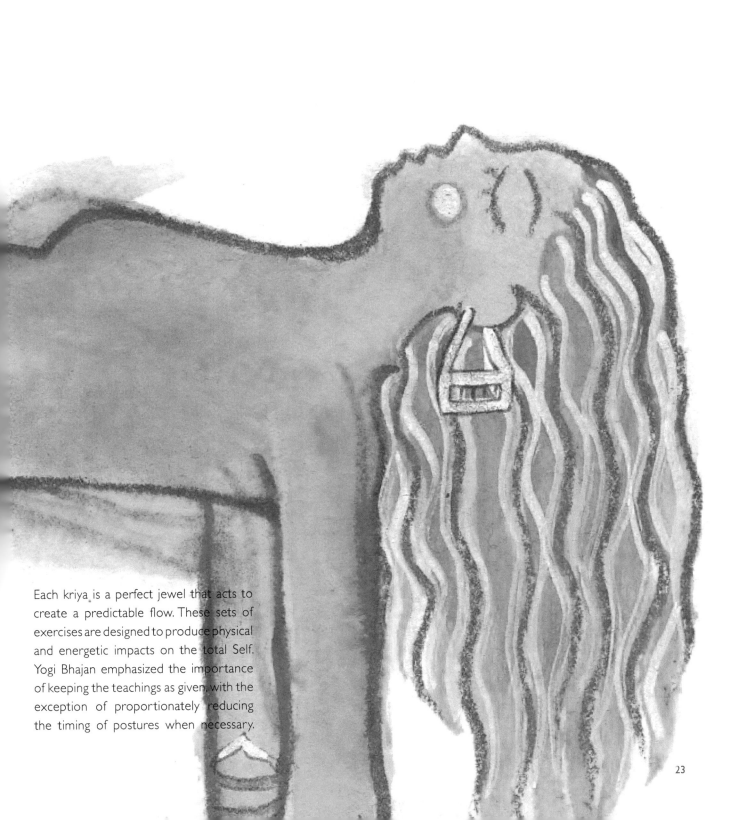

Each kriya is a perfect jewel that acts to create a predictable flow. These sets of exercises are designed to produce physical and energetic impacts on the total Self. Yogi Bhajan emphasized the importance of keeping the teachings as given, with the exception of proportionately reducing the timing of postures when necessary.

GROUNDING: FLEXIBLE BODY, FLEXIBLE MIND - ADVANCED

The First, Second and Third Chakras associated with the rectum, sex organs and Navel Point are thoroughly exercised in this kriya. It gives flexibility of the spine and improves the power of digestion and elimination of waste and toxins. If the set is done every morning for six months, it adjusts the spine so well that many future chiropractic bills will be unnecessary.

Hatha Yoga teaches us to use the body as the bow, asana as the arrow, and the soul the target. ~ BKS Iyengar

1. ARCHER POSE:

From Downward Dog step your right foot forward in-between your hands and ground left heel 45° to the back edge of your mat. Right knee above ankle. Extend right arm parallel, make a fist as if holding a bow pull the left arm back as if pulling the bowstring back to the shoulder. Feel a tension across the chest. Focus eyes to horizon. **3 - 5 minutes**, Repeat left side. **Benefits:** Works on the first chakra with a strong earth connection. Helps develop strength in the legs and the intestines. Stimulates the bones to retain calcium.
11 minutes of Archer Pose on each side is a simple way to build up the Radiant Body.

2. STRETCH POSE VARIATION:

On back, both feet 60cm from the ground. Long deep breathing. **1 - 3 minutes. Modifications:** Hands under buttocks / Raise one leg at a time at equal intervals.
Benefits: Adjusts and strengthens the navel point, your power centre. Tunes-up your nervous and digestive systems. Strengthens the reproduction organs and glands.

3. LOCUST POSE:

Make fists with the hands and put them on the lower abdomen inside the front hip bones near the groin. Keep heels together and legs straight. Lift legs up as high as possible. Breath of Fire. **3 minutes.** Relax. **Modifications:** Cross ankles or do one leg at a time. **Benefits:** Strengthens the kidneys, adrenals, nervous system, navel centre and lower back. For women it helps to prevent build up of tension in the ovaries.

4. BOW POSE:

Hold your ankles, rise up into Bow Pose. Engage abdominal muscles and bring your big toes to touch. Focus tip of your nose. Long Deep Breathing. **2 - 3 minutes.**
Modifications: Interlace your fingers behind you, cross your ankles and lift up as high as you comfortably can.
Benefits: Massages internal organs thereby improving the function of liver, pancreas, small and big intestine. An effective mood elevator because it gets stagnant energy moving.
Caution: back pain, hernia, should practice Dhanurasana with careful supervision.

5. ALTERNATE TOE TOUCH:

Stand with legs spread wide apart, feet parallel, arms stretched out in a T shape. Inhale, exhale, fold and touch the right hand to or toward the left foot or ankle. The left arm is pointing straight up in line with the right hand. Keep legs straight and hips level. Switch sides and continue this alternate motion with long breaths. **Repeat 25 times** on each side.

Benefits: Strengthens the abdominal, upper back, and shoulders, and stretches the hamstrings, calves, hips, lower back, and spine. Allows the heart centre to shine. Relieves anxiety. Gives liver, kidneys and spleen a good rinse, washing toxins out of our systems.

There's nothing which can be more precious in you than your own relationship with your own consciousness. ~ Yogi Bhajan

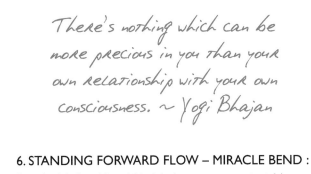

6. STANDING FORWARD FLOW – MIRACLE BEND :

Stand with feet hip width. Inhale, eyes open, stretching arms up to frame your face and gaze toward your palms. Keep your arms straight. Exhale and bend forward from your hips, bending knees slightly. Place the palms flat on the ground, close your eyes. **Continue 25 times.**

Modification: Place your hands on your calves.

Benefits: Calming. As you fold your body the mind draws inward. Helps create length and greater breath awareness in the entire back of the body. Forward flow is good for the entire spine. It unleashes spinal fluid and expands the aura.

7. STANDING SIDE BENDS:

Feet hip distance apart. Stretch arms straight up over head. Inhale. As you exhale arc to the left allowing your left arm to reach toward your left knee.

Right arm stretches over head toward the left. Alternate smoothly from side to side. Continue **25 times on each side.**

Chant: RA MA DA SA, SA SAY SO HUNG in unison with the movement to promote emotional healing and balance.

Benefits: Stretches the intercostal muscles. Stimulates the liver. Left and right side of the body are balanced.

Ida, Pingala. Sun, Moon. Male, Female.

8. WIDE-ANGLE SEATED FORWARD BEND:

Hold big toes of each foot by locking the forefingers around the toe. Thumb pressing the toenail. Keep a firm grip on both toes without pulling toes apart. Inhale, arch up the spine. Exhale, bring your head toward the right knee. Inhale to the original position, and exhale down toward the left knee. **Continue 25 times** on each side. **Modifications:** Sit on the edge of a blanket or foam block / Bend knees slightly. As you move into the forward bend keep the knee caps pointing up toward the ceiling. **Benefits:** Stretches inner thighs and backs of legs. Strengthens the spine. Releases groins. Stimulates lymph nodes in upper chest and pelvic region. Moves stagnant energy in the lower 3 chakras, inspiring creativity.

9. LIFE NERVE STRETCH:

Bring the legs together while holding onto the toes. Press heels firmly down. Inhale. Exhale fold forward from the hips. Keep shoulders soft away from ears. Extend crown of your head toward your feet.

Creating a pumping up/down motion **25 times.**

Modifications: Keep spine lengthened and bend knees slightly.

Benefits: Stretches the spine, shoulders, hamstrings. The main meridian points for every system and organ is along the sciatic nerve. When we work on the life nerve, we are working on everything.

10. PLOUGH POSE:

Lie on your back. Slowly raise legs over the head until they touch the floor. Keep knees straight and point toes away from your head, stretching the heels back. **5 minutes.** There's a tendency to overstretch the neck by pulling the shoulders too far away from the ears. **Modifications:** Bring your feet as close to the floor as you comfortably can.

Benefits: Gives a gentle massage to the abdominal region. Releases nerve "knots in your stomach". Strengthens the colon for proper assimilation of the food and provides relief from various stomach disorders.

11. SHOULDER STAND SERIES:

Raise up into shoulder stand. Support the spine perpendicular to the ground with the hands. Let most of the weight be on the elbows. Hold this position for **3 - 5 minutes.**

Then bring the legs down in back of the head as in plough pose, with legs spread wide apart. Slowly go from this position to shoulder stand **4 times.** Lower the legs and spine rest on the back **30 seconds. Benefits:** Yogi Bhajan talks about this being the ultimate posture to provide health, youth and beauty. It realigns and takes pressure off the internal organs.

12. PLOUGH POSE:

Alternate from plough pose to lying flat on the back. Continue **50 complete times.** Relax for 3 minutes.
Modifications: Raise legs to 90° / alternate leg raises.
Benefits: Good for the circulation, the heart, stomach, and lungs. Aids in the flexibility of the spine.

13. SAT KRIYA:

Sit on the heels with the arms over head and the palms together. Chant "Sat" and pull the navel point in, chant "Nam" and release it. Continue powerfully with a steady rhythm for **5 minutes.** Keep stretching up from your armpits and recommit to the exercise if you feel yourself fading.
Inhale, apply mulbandh and draw the energy up the spine to the brow point. Relax.
Modifications: Sit in easy pose / Bring mudra to navel centre.
Benefits: Page 48

14. GURPRANAM:

Place the forehead on the ground and stretch the arms overhead, keeping the palms together. Meditate at the brow point by silently projecting the sounds, "Sa Ta Na Ma." Continue for **31 minutes.**
THIS IS THE ULTIMATE POSTURE OF DEVOTION.

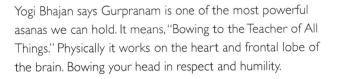

Yogi Bhajan says Gurpranam is one of the most powerful asanas we can hold. It means, "Bowing to the Teacher of All Things." Physically it works on the heart and frontal lobe of the brain. Bowing your head in respect and humility.

The posture is said to have an interesting emotional effect as it brings about a sense of grieving and sadness. This feeling comes about because you are actually grieving the loss of your own self. You lose a part of yourself when surrendering to something bigger than you.

The moment you touch your soul, you become fearless. ~ Yogi Bhajan

15. EASY POSE:

Inhale, raise both arms over the head bringing the backs of the hands together. Exhale, lower the arms letting just the fingertips lightly touch the floor. **5 minutes.**
Benefits: Flushes lymphatic system. Gives thymus region a boost. Energetically helps with connection to the heart chakra.

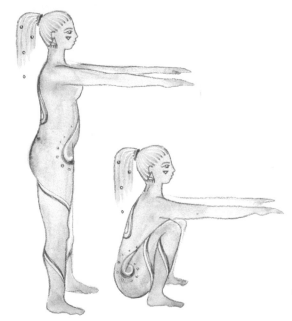

16. DYNAMIC CROW SQUAT:

Stand up and extend the arms straight forward parallel to the ground. Begin **25 squats** into crow squat.
Keep spine straight and the feet flat.
Knees steady and moving in the same direction as feet.
Modifications: Stand with your heels on a rolled mat or blanket. Come down half way if all the way is not possible.
Benefits: Strengthens nerves and increase cardio capability. Strengthens legs. Realigns colon. Good hip opener. Stimulates chakras 1 & 2. Grounding earth posture.

There's nothing which can be more precious in you than your own relationship with your own consciousness. ~ Yogi Bhajan

17. CAT-COW:

Come onto your hands and knees. Arch your spine down and raise the head with the inhale. Exhale, arch the spine up and lower the head. **5 minutes.**
Benefits: Increases flexibility of the neck, shoulders, and spine. Irons out tension build-up in the spine.
The fast cat-cow pumps a great flux of cerebrospinal fluid through your system. Gradually increase speed.

18. RELAX: for **15 to 30 minutes** on the back.

Cover the body with a blanket to keep from getting cold.

COMMENTS:

This set is an example of a series which would not be given in a normal 90 minute Kundalini yoga class. It is for students who want to eject residual poisons and drugs from the muscle tissue. It can be adapted to a regular class by keeping the time of the exercises to 1-2 minutes and adding rest periods between the postures.

CREATING: GLANDS, CIRCULATION AND THE MEDITATIVE MIND

"If you do not have self reliance, what do you have? You can cross mountains, oceans, tragedies and difficulties with only one thing, self-reliance. Fear not my dear ones: the antidote to fear is self-reliance."
Keep your focus on the breath as well as the dynamic, rhythmic movement for you to experience the benefits of this Kriya.

Make sure your body is warmed up before beginning this kriya.

I. BRIDGE SQUAT:

Come into a squat. Place your palms flat on the floor behind you. Inhale, lift your hips up into a modified bridge pose.
In this position, begin swinging the head up and down at a fast pace with Breath of Fire for **15 seconds.**
Continue Breath of Fire, raise and lower your buttocks rapidly and powerfully. **2 minutes.**
Benefits: This exercise works on the thyroid and parathyroid and adjusts the spine. Strengthens glandular system, and navel point.

2. BACK PLATFORM:

Support your entire weight of your body on your heels and palms. Create a straight line from head to toes. Begin alternate leg lifts, inhaling and exhaling as one leg alternately goes up and down. Move as fast as you can. **2 minutes.**
Modifications: Bend knees into Tabletop Pose and alternately lift legs. If you have problems with your wrists or shoulders come down onto your shoulders into Bridge Pose.
Benefits: Strengthens your back body while simultaneously opening the heart chakra. Builds willpower and grit to give you the ability to overcome challenges and obstacles in life.

3. TABLETOP POSE:

Feet and palms are flat on the floor. Knees bent and hips arched up, body is in a straight line from head to knees. Begin rolling your neck around in circles.
Inhale as your neck rolls round in one direction, then powerfully exhale as you roll your neck in the opposite direction. **I minute.**
Benefits: Releases tension in the neck. Stretches the front side of your body and the shoulders, and strengthens the arms, wrists and the legs. Improves your posture and gives you a boost of energy.

4. RELAX: 2 minutes.

5. LEG RAISES:

Lie down on your back. Point the toes and bring the feet together, heels touching. Hands relaxed by your sides. Consciously relax the body from the navel point up. Keeping the toes pointed, SLOWLY raise the legs to 90° as you inhale. Lower them as you exhale. Throughout the exercise the body should be mentally divided into two areas from the navel point up is totally relaxed. **6 minutes.**
Benefits: Good for circulation, the heart, stomach and lungs.

6. OPEN AND CLOSE:

On the back, bring the legs up to 90° close together. Inhale and open the legs wide as you can. Exhale, close them again. Continue. Knees straight and toes pointed. **6 minutes.**
Modifications: Hands underneath buttocks for support.
Benefits: Works on abdominal toning. Gives endurance and integrates the release of sexual energy into the other body systems. According to Yogi Bhajan, it is good to create a habit of practicing a kriya like this frequently. If you do it while you are vital, your body will not fail you when you are older!

7. LEG KICKS:

Still on your back, inhale legs to 90°. Exhale quickly bring heels down to strike the buttocks with force.
Continue at a very fast pace for **2 minutes.**
Benefits: Stimulates navel center. Opens life nerve channel.

8. CROSS CRAWLS:

Begin alternate arm/leg lifts. Inhale, raise the right leg and the left arm to 90°. Exhale and lower them. Change sides. Continue for **2 minutes.** Move as fast as you can. Keep the legs and arms straight. **Benefits:** Charges the navel centre and helps with the correct functioning of your digestive system. Balances our brain hemispheres which balances our energy.

9. SIT LIKE A YOGI:

In easy pose, hands in gyan mudra on the knees.
Chant from your navel: **HARA HARA HARA HARA HAREE HAR. 4 minutes. Benefits:** This vibration builds a sense of self-reliance. Har is the creative vessel for our truth to flow.

10. EASY POSE:

Hold your hands in front of your body at neck level, palms facing each other. In a monotone, extremely rapidly, chant **HAR HAR HAR HAR.** Simultaneously move your hands back and forth in opposite directions. Chant powerfully: move fast. After **30 seconds.** Inhale deeply and hold the breath in for 20 seconds. Exhale, relax. "Feel yourself to be blessed."
Benefits: Movement of the arms provide a workout for the lymphatic, immune and circulatory system.

11. RELAX: 10 minutes.

EMPOWERING: NAVEL CHAKRA AND ELIMINATION

The buildup of wastes in the digestive tract prevents good absorption of nutrients and provides a breeding ground for bacteria and illness. If elimination is blocked in the main channels, your body will try to expel the toxins via the skin in pimples, rashes, boils, etc.

This kriya works out the entire eliminative system. Then the sexual energy and breath energy are stimulated and circulated. Finally exercises 15 to 17 raise the energy to the higher centres.

1. PUSH PULL:

Lie on the back. Lift both legs 30° off the ground with the toes pointing forward. Alternately draw your knees to the chest with long deep breaths. Keep the legs parallel to the ground. **1 - 2 minutes.**

Benefits: Charges navel centre. Improves digestive functioning.

2. LEG LIFT:

On back, palms down by your side. Inhale, lift legs up 90° exhale, lower the legs. Continue at a rapid pace. **1 minute.** Rest for **30 seconds.** Repeat this sequence 2 more times.

Modifications: Keep hands under buttocks for support. Alternate legs. **Benefits:** Strengthens navel chakra. Balances the flow of life force. Good for elimination and balancing flow of Prana and Apana.

3. COBRA POSE VARIATION:

Cobra Pose start to kick your buttocks with alternate heels. Exhale each time the heels strike the buttocks. **2 minutes.**

Modification: Keep elbows bent or forearms on the floor.

Benefits: Tones the deeper layers of the abdominal region. Stimulates kidneys to detox. Regenerates adrenals. Facilitates the flow of the Kundalini energy. Opens life nerve channel.

4. ROCKING BOW:

Reach back for the ankles and stretch up into Bow Pose. Look toward the sky. Roll back and forth on the stomach. Inhale back, exhale forward. **2 minutes.**

Modification: Hold pose with long deep breathing / Hold onto your ankles. Inhale up, exhale lower down.

Benefits: Massages internal organs.

5. SPINAL ROLLS:

Lie on the back. Clasp the knees to the chest. Roll forward and back on the spine. **2 minutes.**

Benefits: Massages the spine, in particular the lower back. Counter to previous pose.

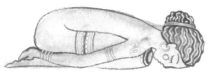

6. BABY POSE:

Sit on the heels. Bring your forehead to the floor and hold on to heels. **1 - 2 minutes.**

Benefits: Relaxes your muscles on the front of the body while gently stretching the muscles of the back torso. Calms the body, mind and spirit. Stimulates the third eye point.

7. STRETCH POSE:

On your back. Lift your heels, head and shoulders 15cm. Gaze at your toes with Breath of Fire. **2 minutes.**

Modification: One leg at a time alternating every few seconds.

Benefits: Stimulates circulation while toning the abdominal muscles and igniting will power.

8. LOCUST POSE:

Lie on the stomach with the arms stretched forward. Hands in Venus Lock. Lift the legs and arms off the ground; the arms hug the ears. Breath of Fire. **1.5 minutes.**

Modification: One leg at a time or try crossing your ankles.

Benefits: Firms buttocks. Strengthens kidneys, adrenals, nervous system and lower back. Helps to move through blocks when nothing else seems to be working.

9. STANDING SIDE BEND:

Standing Mountain Pose, arms relaxed along the sides and begin to swing like a pendulum from side to side. Bend to the left inhale and right with the exhale. Move gracefully. **2 minutes.**

Benefits: Stretches the intercostal muscles. Stimulates liver to detox. Balances our sun and moon energy.

10. STANDING TWIST:

Begin twisting from side to side. Twist left, extend the left arm parallel to the ground and place the right hand on your heart; twist right, extend the right arm parallel to the ground and place the left hand on heart.

Continuous motion with deep breaths. **2 minutes.**

Benefits: Keeps fascia healthy and lubricated. The gesture of palm on your heart is grounding and centering.

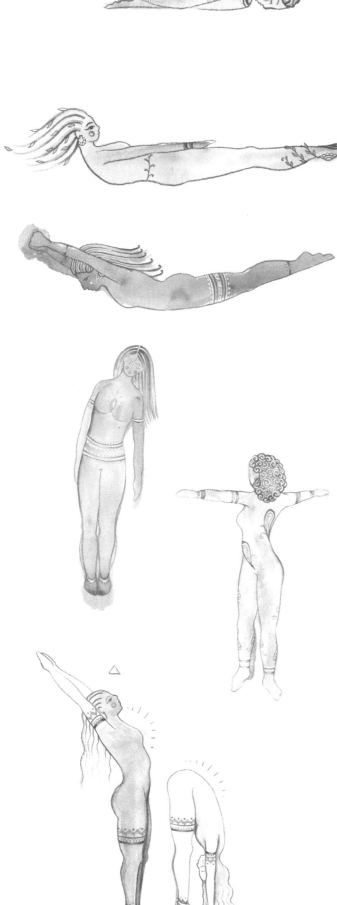

11. MIRACLE BEND:

Bend forward with the knees straight. Touch the palms flat on the ground. Straighten up with the arms together, thumbs hooked, and lean back as far as possible. Hold the position for 10 seconds. As you lean back, the breath will automatically come in; as you bend forward, the breath will automatically release. **Repeat 10 - 20 times.**

Modifications: Bend knees.

Benefits: Releases the hamstrings. Opens upper back region and lungs. Opens our heart chakra to help release stagnation and blocked emotions.

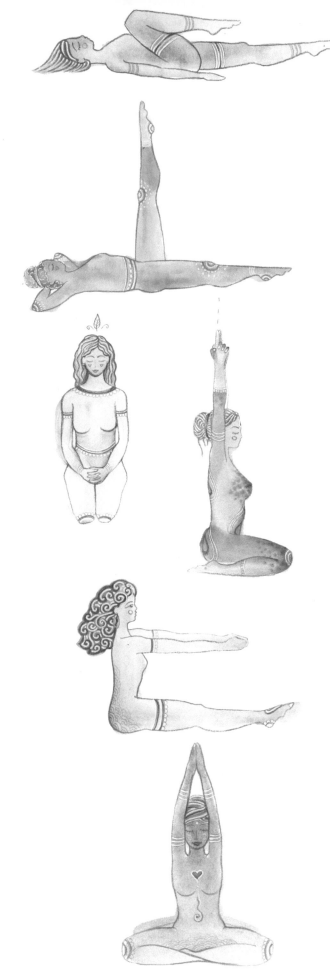

12. PUSH PULL:

Lie on the back. Lift both legs 30° off the ground with the toes pointing forward. Alternately draw your knees to the chest with long deep breaths. Keep the legs parallel to the ground. **1-2 minutes.**
Benefits: Recharges navel centre.

13. ALTERNATE LEG LIFTS:

Stay on the back and place the hands in Venus Lock on the back of the neck under hair. Rapidly raise and lower alternate legs to 90°. Inhale up. Exhale down. **2 minutes.**
Modifications: Place hands under your buttocks if there is strain in your lower back.
Benefits: Strengthens and tones abdominal region.
Balances the left and right hemispheres of brain so that we can feel strong, centered and focused.

14. MEDITATE:

Sit on the heels with Venus Lock in your lap. Concentrate on the breath and the mantra: Inhale SAT, exhale NAM. Continue for **3 minutes.**

15. SAT KRIYA:

Sit on the heels. Raise the hands overhead in Venus Lock with Jupiter fingers extended. Chant SAT verbally and pull Mulbandha. Chant NAM and relax. Continue rhythmically for **2 minutes** and then inhale, exhale, and apply Mulbandha.

16. STAFF POSE:

Sit up with the legs out straight. Raise the arms parallel to the ground. Begin Breath of Fire powerfully for **2 minutes.**
Benefits: Strengthens all major core muscles, improves posture and increases stamina.

17. EASY POSE:

Raise the arms overhead with palms together, arms hugging the ears. Close the eyes and meditate at the Third Eye Point.
Chant: EK ONG KAAR SAT NAAM SIREE WHA-HAY GUROO. 3-5 minutes.

This is a potent Ashtang (8 sounds) mantra which helps transform emotions from negative to positive. Each sound vibrates and interacts with a different chakra as well as within our aura allowing us to feel more receptive and centered.

18. RELAX: 10 minutes

That infinity, that God, that purity, that power, that pure power is in your navel point. You can't buy it, you can't sell it, and I cannot give it to you. But I give you technological knowledge from which you can initiate it. So it will start working for you. I am not saying there will be no problems. But you will be untouched. You can sit like a lotus in the muddy waters and enjoy life. That is the power of the third chakra. It gives you instant, infinite experience of your life. No time can measure it. ~ Yogi Bhajan

COMPASSION: THE ESSENCE OF SELF

This series of exercises guides the pranic life force through the body to the heart centre, opening the heart so that you can give and receive love without fear, anger or resentment. This state of compassion is the essence of self. When feeling weighted down, this kriya can help you sense the broader reality of which you are a part. All possibilities open to you when you live from the essence of Self. Physically this kriya releases tensions, strengthens digestion and opens the lungs.

Make sure your body is warmed up before beginning this kriya.

1. ARM CIRCLES:

Easy Pose. Extend arms to the front and slightly to the sides. Form a "V" with the body. Arms straight out from the shoulders. Hands extended. Palms facing down. Rotate arms backwards in large circles. Keep the arms positioned so that the circles are in front and slightly out to the sides. Breath of Fire. Make this an energetic exercise by gradually increasing the power of the breath as you rotate your arms faster and wider. Feel the space around your body becoming charged. **4 minutes.**

Benefits: Arm movement stimulates the heart centre and opens the lungs. It amplifies our magnetic field.

2. ROCKING BOW:

Lie on the stomach and assume Bow Pose: Reach back take hold of the ankles and stretch up by creating tension between the arms and legs. Rock back and forth from the shoulders to the knees, coordinating the motion with a powerful Breath of Fire, so powerful that it feels as though fire were coming from the nostrils. **1 minute.** Relax briefly.

Modifications: Interlace your hands behind your back and raise your legs as high as possible.

Benefits: Massages internal organs, especially the digestive organs. The breath and movement invigorates your entire being, stimulating the movement of energy to the heart.

3. SPINAL ROCK:

Hold your knees to your chest and rock back and forth on the spine in conjunction with Breath of Fire. **1 minute.**

Benefits: Strengthens the lower back. Massaging spine gently from the neck to the base. Removes tension in the back and balances the flow of sexual energy with navel energy.

4. CROW SQUATS:

Stand with feet hip width apart. Feet turned slightly outward. Exhale and crouch down. Spine as straight as possible. Inhale and return to the standing position. Continue for **26 x squats.**
Modifications: Stand with your heels on a rolled mat.
The wider you spread your feet, the easier it is.
Benefits: Increases flexibility in the groin and hips. Good for healthy knee and ankle joints. Tones and massages the elimination system. This is a primal pose which draws upon the earth element for grounding. Gives a sense of security, connectivity to nature and down-to-earth thinking.

5. ARM CIRCLES: Repeat the first exercise for **1 - 2 minutes.**

6. ESSENCE OF SELF MEDITATION:

Sitting in Easy Pose, cross the hands at the centre of the chest over the heart centre. Close the eyes. Remain focused and meditate for **5 - 31 minutes.** If available, meditate with or sing a divine, uplifting mantra.

7. RELAX: 10 minutes

Drop any self—limitations.
Surrender the self to the Self.
In this expanded awareness you will
experience your essence.

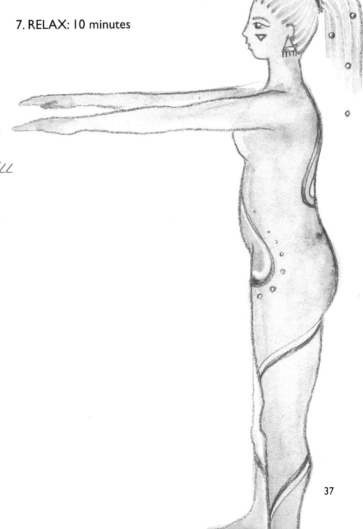

VIBRATING: CONSCIOUS COMMUNICATION

Communication is the art of listening. In this Kriya we activate the yin state of balance attained in the heart space and move it up to a yang state of self expression. "The highest most effective energy of this planet is the word. We must consciously understand the power of the word and apply the whole mind behind the word. Then we create the word which can create the whole world for us."

Make sure your body is warmed up before beginning this kriya.

1. HAMMER:

Bring your left hand into a fist and right hand wraps around it. Keep the elbow straight and begin to pump the arms up and down 60°. **5 minutes.**

Feel your shoulder blades warming up as you hammer with a rhythm. Inject power into the movement.

To end: Relax hands down to knees. Observe the heat generated in your body.

Benefits: Strengthens aura and upper torso. Increases intake of prana.

2. LIE ON YOUR BACK:

Spread your legs far apart. Bring your hands in Venus Lock under your neck. Lift left leg 2 feet above ground and hold with Long Deep Breathing. **1 minute.** Keep naval engaged. Engage entire pelvic region. Change to right side. Repeat entire sequence.

Benefits: Strengthens navel. Opens heart.

3. BREATH SEQUENCE:

Easy pose. Block right nostril and begin inhaling and exhaling through left nostril **3 minutes.** Then right nostril breath **3 minutes.** Inhale left nostril. Exhale right. **3 minutes.** Rapidly inhale right, exhale left with Breath of Fire. **3 minutes.**

Benefits: Taking command of the breath gives you new sense of ease and control over where you direct your mind.

4. STRETCH POSE:

Head and feet raised 15cm. Hands reaching toward toes. Eyes gazing at feet. Breath of Fire. **3 minutes.** Relax. Repeat 2 more times. **Modification:** Alternate one leg at a time on the floor. Hold with long deep breathing if you are in your moon cycle.

Benefits: Harnesses and concentrates your "Chi", the energy that is naturally at your navel centre. Resets the nervous system and strengthens the abdominal area. Rejuvenates and purifies the blood. Boosts resolve and self-esteem. Practice Stretch Pose to stay centred.

5. LIFE NERVE STRETCH SITTING:

Sit on left heel and stretch out the right leg. Hold onto your right foot with both hands. Inhale lift your head and heart. Exhale fold down. Continue **1 minute** each side
Modification: Hold onto the extended leg if you cannot reach your foot. Bring heel to your inner groin.
Benefits: Strengthens leg muscles and lower back.

6. GAS POSE:

On back hug knees to chest. Breath of Fire. **2 Minutes.**
Benefits: Targets the digestive organs and provides gas relief. Sets navel point and stimulates the apana, which helps your digestive system relax and release.

7. STRETCH VARIATION:

Arms parallel to floor lean back 60° from ground. Breath of Fire. **2 minutes.**
Modifications: Start in staff pose and gradually lean backwards. **Benefits:** Power in navel region stimulates movement up toward your heart.

8. EASY POSE:

Look down into you heart. Apply Jalandhar Bhanda. Open and lengthen the back of your neck. Long Deep Breath. **6 minutes.**
Benefits: Draws all the generated navel energy up to the higher centres.

9. CAMEL POSE:

Long deep breath. **2 minutes.** Release. **Repeat 2 more times.**
Modifications: Hands on hips or interlaced behind the back.
Benefits: Creates maximum compression of the spine, which stimulates the nervous system. Improves flexibility of the neck. Stretches the throat and parathyroid. Opens rib cage to give more space to the lungs. The heart stores the emotions of stress, fear and anxiety. By opening up the heart chakra, you begin to release these emotions.

10. EASY POSE:

Hand in Gyan Mudra, Breath of Fire. **2 minutes.**
Relax for **1 minute.** Repeat.
Benefits: Strengthen the lungs, purifies the blood, enhances oxygenation of the body. Regular practice boosts the immune system. Burns up karma.

11. EASY POSE:

Interlace hands behind neck in Venus Lock. Stretch elbows back as you inhale. Exhale point elbows forward. **2 minutes.**
Benefits: Directs all the energies from the previous exercises into balancing the throat chakra and thyroid.

12. RELAX: 10 minutes.

INTUITION: KNOWING WHAT TO DO

"All living matter is comprised of five elements: earth, air, fire, water and ether. These are known as the 5 Tattvas. Normally Breath of Fire creates a neutral state. Here, however, the movement of the hands creates that differentiation and synchronizes the hemispheres as well.
This is a very powerful set of exercises to practice every day." Yogi Bhajan.

I. VIRASAN:

Sit in Virasan and bring the palms into prayer mudra at the sternum. (Place the palms together at the heart centre.)

Virasan: Known as the warriors meditation position as it is a seated position ideal for meditating as well as a ready position for lunging into action.

Benefits: Brings the mind into focus. Opens heart. Stimulates circulation to cleanse the blood of disease. Conquers laziness and depression. Improves digestion and elimination.

Modification: Right leg extended on ground.
Left heel pressed into right thigh/groin.

Notes: Sitting with the right knee up ignites a sunny digestive fire. Projecting upwards - Stimulating.
Sitting with the left shin down promotes the lunar elimination in the colon. Grounding downwards - Releasing.

a) Extend left arm 60° out to the side. Elbow straight.
Begin to rapidly move the left hand up and down at the wrist.
Coordinate the movement with Breath of Fire. **3 minutes.**

b) Switch arms and continue for **3 minutes.**

Benefits:
a) Helps differentiate the left from the right hemispheres of the brain.
b) Helps differentiate the right from the left hemispheres of the brain.

c) Extend both arms out to 60° and continue the movement with both hands. **3 minutes.** Visualize yourself flying high in the sky. Pass through each of the five elements in turn and totally identify with each one.
Ether - Air - Fire - Water - Earth - Feel the difference between each tattva then return to Ether again.
Spend about **15 seconds on each tattva** and pay special attention when you experience Ether a second time.

Benefits: Synchronises both hemispheres of the brain and brings all the tattvas into a state of balance.

2. EASY POSE:

Make fists of both hands with the thumbs tucked inside. Hold them palm down in front of the heart centre. Rotate the fists rapidly around each other in coordination with Breath of Fire for **1 minute.** Keep the wrists firm.

Benefits: Strengthens the aura to induce a physical experience of elevation and clarity. Squeezing the thumbs (ego) helps you to mentally experience what is beyond the body.

3. RELAX 5 minutes.

Never be right or wrong, always be neutral. Speak not through the positive mind or the negative mind, but from the neutral mind. And whenever you have to confront a calamity or a pleasure, take the altitude. Adjust the attitude. Do not react right away. ~ Yogi Bhajan

CONNECTION: GLOWING FROM THE INSIDE OUT

The Pineal Gland is said to be the highest gland and believed to be our connection to God. It is also said to be the "Angel" Gland that connects us to that realm. This is a powerful kriya that focuses on expanding our consciousness, awakening the neutral mind, the sixth and seventh chakras.

I. SHAKTI POSE 6TH CHAKRA:

Interlace fingers in Venus Lock. Palms facing down 15-20 cm above the top of your head. Hold the lock tightly and try pull fingers apart. Arms are rounded. Eyes closed looking in and up toward your palms through the crown of your head. Long, Deep Breathing for **2.5 minutes.**
Then meditate with your hands in Gyan Mudra for **5 minutes.**
Benefits: Venus Lock redirects sexual energy while balancing the glandular system. This full body mudra stretches through the belly, shoulders and armpits. Energising the second chakra to open the third eye and crown. It is said if your third eye is open, you can see your destiny. Intuition is a penetrative quality of the mind.

2. SHAKTI POSE 7TH CHAKRA:

Same as previous exercise but with the thumbs extended straight back thumbprint meeting thumbprint. Long, Deep Breathing for **2.5 minutes.** Eyes focused up through the crown of your head, sahasrara. Then meditate with your hands in Gyan Mudra for **5 minutes.**
Benefits: The thumbs relate to the earth element, the ego. This mudra establishes an appropriate relationship between the ego and the infinite self. It works with your connection to the divine. When the crown is open you are connected to everything. Feeling a sense of ecstasy beyond words.
The pineal gland relates to our circadian rhythms and regulates sleep. An active seventh chakra gives us access to dimensions beyond the mind.

3. SHAKTI POSE 8TH CHAKRA:

In the same position, thumbs clasped and index fingers raised straight up. Create tension between your fingers. Eyes closed looking up again through the crown of your head. Long, Deep Breathing for **2.5 minutes.**
Benefits: The index fingers relate to the planet Jupiter to expand your horizons. Activates the aura, how you project into the world.

4. FUNNEL:

Still sitting, raise your arms up to 60°, spread your fingers wide apart. Visualise you are a funnel and decide what to bring into your experience. Focus your eyes at the brow point. Begin breath of fire. **3 - 5 minutes.**

Benefits: When our radiance is bright, wherever we go, people will feel healed by our presence. (Dalai Lama).

The strength behind communication is in its quality, not in its quantity. Your talk should be that of quality, not of quantity. You should use small sentences which say a lot. Or you should say a lot in small sentences. ~ Yogi Bhajan

5. RELAX IN EASY POSE:

Bring hands to gyan mudra. Eyes closed, focused at the crown. Have no thoughts. Feel part of everything. Feel that you are the universe. Time open.

INFINITE: SWIMMING THROUGH THE PRANIC OCEAN

This kriya is a powerful life lesson that can propel you to grow immensely on your path of self-cultivation. Cross over the stormy ocean of difficult emotions of pain into greater, deep, calm waters of clarity and self-awareness.

1. SWIMMING:

This special breath exercise is called "Swimming through the Pranic ocean". Sit in easy pose and move the arms like you are swimming.

Create a smooth, circular swimming motion that moves the shoulders, rib cage, and back muscles. Create a powerful Breath of Fire through an open mouth in rhythm with the arm motion. Keep the back molars together so the breath sounds like a powerful, pulsing hiss. Imagine you are swimming through all your unresolved emotions. **13 Minutes.**

Benefits: Immune booster. Breath helps to resolve emotional scars. Release in the shoulders. Tension in shoulders is related to the 5th Chakra. This imbalance is caused by an inability to let go or forgive. Energetically sadness and grief is associated with the lungs. Transform grief into conscious knowledge of your feelings.

2. BACK PLATFORM POSE:

Come into back platform pose. Keep your body straight, especially your knees. Let your neck relax backwards without compressing your neck. After **2 Minutes**, form a circle with your mouth and breathe strongly. Use the diaphragm to drive the breath. This is not a breath of fire from the navel, it is a "pancreas" breath that is focused near the sternum and diaphragm. **2 Minutes.**

Modification: Bend one leg at a time with equal intervals.

Benefits: Strengthens the back body. Opens the heart center. Balances the thyroid. Energetically, the Pancreas has to do with the ability to allow "sweetness" into our lives. When the energy in the Pancreas is weak, we have trouble receiving love and also don't believe that we are worthy of love.

3. RELAX: Deeply relax. Let go. Love yourself. **3 - 5 Minutes.**

4. SEATED DANCING:

Come into a sitting position and dance. This spreads the energy equally to all parts of the body. Create waves of gratitude and love. Express yourself freely. **5 Minutes.**

Benefits: Helps us to peel off our mask. To shed skins. To crack moulds and to experience infinity.

5. RELAX: 5 - 10 minutes.

Your immune system works for you, but do you work for your immune system?
Your heart works for you. Do you work for your heart? Your organs work for you. Do you work for each of your organs?
I don't think you have asked yourself questions like these. YB October 23, 1985

TRANSFORMING LOWER TO HIGHER - ADVANCED

If the energy in the lower triangle of chakras is not balanced and able to transform to higher energy frequencies, man is a slave to his hunger, thirst, and sexuality. This set stimulates the energy of the lower triangle and transforms this energy into the higher brain structures: pituitary, pineal, memory gland. The rest between exercises is short and all breathing should be done with enthusiasm.

Make sure your body is warmed up before beginning this kriya.

Turn on your courage
To enter the fire of transformation.

1. CAMEL POSE:

Come onto your knees hip-width apart. Bring your hands on your lower back, fingers pointing up. Keep hips over knees. Internally rotate thighs. Lift sternum. Expand rib cage. Navel engaged. Spine long, and chin tucked. Lower hands toward your heels. Relax head and neck back. Third eye focus or tip of nose. Breath of Fire. **3 minutes.**
Inhale, hold the breath for 10 seconds.
Remain in the same pose, begin SAT KRIYA: (page 48) draw your navel in while exhaling with a vocal **SAT** and relaxing **NAM**, take a short inhale. **3 minutes. To end:** Exit as you entered. Lead with your heart to bring your body up.
Sit in Rock pose. **Modifications:** Hands on hips and lift through the breast bone or curl the toes under for extra length and hold onto heels. Interlace hands behind back.
Benefits: Works on all the chakras simultaneously.
Helps curb obsessive behaviours around food and substances via stimulating the endocrine and digestive system.
Helps to alleviate depression. Strengthens the spine, improves posture and releases tension around the ovaries.

2. Bring your forehead forward to the ground. Interlace fingers in Venus lock on the back. Raise the feet and forelegs off the ground near the buttocks. Balance and meditate at the brow point. Create a perfect balance between head and knees. Elevate your heart by using the Venus lock to extend your elbows to open your chest. Make sure the patella is not carrying the weight. **3 minutes.** Long Deep Breathing.
Modification: Hands on floor if you feel strain in your neck.
Benefits: Releases energy to the brain giving clarity of thought and clear sparkling eyes. Stimulates the crown chakra.

3. Remain in posture and place your hands under your shoulders, extend the right leg straight back and up to 60°. Begin to kick right buttock with your heel. Breath of Fire. **2 minutes** each side. Focus eyes on the Crown Chakra, tongue pressing the roof of the mouth.

4. CELIBATE POSE:

Move straight into celibate pose with buttocks on the ground between the heels. Long, deep, slow breathing. **2 minutes.**
IN YOUR MIND DO THE IDEAL POSTURE FOR YOU.
Modifications: Sit on a folded blanket or bolster.
Rock pose, on your heels or Easy Pose. **Benefits:** Increases potency by transforming sexual energy to your higher centres.

Sat Nam is the bij, or seed, mantra. It is small and potent. Great things grow from it. ~ Yogi Bhajan

5. RECLINING HERO:

Stay seated between heels and recline onto your back Lengthen tailbone toward your knees. Soften front ribs back. Press firmly down on shin bones point your toes straight back.

SAT KRIYA 3 - 5 minutes.

Modifications: Prop up on forearms and elbows, if available use a bolster to support your back / Supta Baddha Konasana.

Benefits: Improves digestion. Stretches quadriceps. Helps sciatica. Relieves sleeping disorders. Exposing and expanding the front body leads you into a space of full openness. Allow emotions to move through your body.

6. CAMEL POSE:

Repeat Camel pose. Long, deep, slow breathing. **2 minutes.** Begin Breath of Fire **2 minutes.**

Go to the edge to create a sweat.

To end: Inhale, hold briefly, exhale, slowly come to sit on your heals. Yogi Bhajan said that any pain occurred during this posture is a result of a bad attitude to life.

7. GURPRANAM:

Bring forehead to the ground, extend the arms straight with the palms together. Elbows hug the ears. **3 minutes.**

Benefits: Stimulates pineal and pituitary.

Gurpranam is a powerful chakra balancing exercise for our energy field. It is a simple, but incredibly transformative chakra yoga pose. The position is the body language of surrender, making the statement, both inwardly and outwardly, that **"I bow and allow the flow of the divine."**

When the world pushes you to your knees, you're in the perfect position to pray. Rumi

8. STRETCH POSE SEQUENCE:

Head lifted and feet 15cm off the ground, toes pointed. Breath of Fire. **3 minutes.** Inhale deeply and lift the knees to the heart. Exhale and extend legs parallel the ground. Continue with long, deep, slow breathing for **2 minutes.**

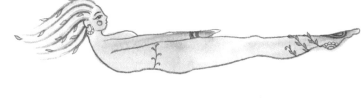

Modifications: Place hands under your buttocks. Or raise one leg at a time at equal intervals.

Benefits: Many imbalances can be corrected by strengthening our navel centre. There are 72 000 nerve channels carrying the life force of the body through this centre. When we pump our navel we are actually pumping from a centre where the thousands of nerves come together. The nerve endings will be stimulated and the energy will consolidate at this point. Stretch Pose stimulates circulation, lengthens and tones the abdominal muscles. Releases energy at the navel point.

The body is my temple, asanas are my prayers.
~ BKS Iyengar

9. SHOULDER STAND:

Rise up into shoulder stand. Support the spine with your hands. Fingers and thumbs pointing up. Put your weight on your elbows, upper arms and shoulders.
Create a vertical line from your shoulders to your toes. Breath of Fire. **3 minutes.**

Modifications: Rest your weight on your shoulders and support your lower back with your hands. Raise your legs as high as possible / legs up at 90° against the wall.

Benefits: Opens the digestion and elimination of the intestines. Stimulates the thyroid and parathyroid for the metabolism and health of our bones. Reduces fatigue and alleviates insomnia.

10. PLOUGH POSE:

Lower the legs over the head to the ground in plough pose with the arms straight back. Breath of Fire. **3 minutes.**
Raise up in to shoulder stand. Breath of Fire. **3 minutes.**

Modifications: Bring your feet to a prop or the wall if you cannot comfortably bring them to the floor and keep your hands on your back to help support your mid spine.

Benefits: Calms the mind. Aids flexibility of the spine. Stimulates abdominal organs, and the thyroid gland. Reduces stress, fatigue, backache and can help you get to sleep!

11. REPEAT STRETCH POSE SEQUENCE NO 8.

12. LOCUST POSE VARIATION:

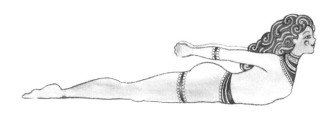

Immediately roll onto the stomach and come into Locust pose with your hands in Venus Lock behind your back. Breath of Fire. **3 minutes.** Relax.

Benefits: Helps relieve stress by opening the heart. Strengthens the kidneys, adrenals, nervous system, navel centre and lower back. Promotes circulation to upper back.

13. LOCUST KICK:

Keep chest relaxed on the ground, begin to kick the buttocks with alternate legs. Keep chin on floor. Eyes closed rolled downwards to the centre of the chin. **3 minutes.**

Benefits: Cooling and calming. Opens life nerve channel.

14. ROCKING BOW POSE:

Hold ankles and arch up into bow pose. Keep your knees no more than hip width apart. Rock back and forth. **2 minutes.**

Modifications: Interlace hands behind your back, lift chest, bend knees.

Benefits: The anti-aging exercise in Kundalini Yoga. Yogi Bhajan says rocking 20 minutes a day will keep you young for life! Massages internal organs. Balances prana and apana at the navel centre. Flushes the lymph nodes. Balances your aura by distributing energy.

*Remember you have the power,
through the sweat of your brow,
to make everything wrong, right.*
~ Yogi Bhajan

*Besides helping cleanse the subconscious
mind, this mantra balances the
hemispheres of the brain, bringing
compassion and patience to the one who
meditates on it. ~ Yogi Bhajan*

15. COBRA POSE:

Place your hands under your shoulders. Stretch and lengthen through your lower back and legs. Clip your toenails down toward the floor. Relax and release your shoulders away from your ears and rise up into Cobra Pose.
Breath of Fire. **3 minutes.**
Modifications: Rest on your forearms with your elbows directly under your shoulders.
Benefits: Strengthens our lower back, kidneys and spine. Stretches chest, lungs, shoulders and abdomen. Invigorates the heart and is a mood uplifter.
Compromised kidneys make us retracted and fearful.

16. BUTTERFLY POSE:

Sit up and bring the soles of the feet together. Release the head of the thigh bones toward the floor. Allow knees to naturally follow. Interlace your fingers around the baby toe side of your feet. Rock back and forth in rhythm with the chant. **5 - 31 minutes.**
Modifications: Sit on a high support.
Benefits: Stretches the inner thighs, groins, and knees. Sparks the creative energy flow in the second chakra. There is a significant relationship between the Fifth and Second chakra both having a strong creative force: the spoken word is the beginning of creation and the seed of creation lies in the second chakra.

GOBINDAY, MUKUNDAY, UDHARAY, APARAY, HARIANG, KARIANG, NIRNAMAY, AKAMAY.
Sustainer, Liberator, Enlightener, Infinite,
Destroyer, Creator, Nameless, Desireless.
The **Guru Gaitri Mantra**, is a powerful tool for moving through difficult situations. These are the 8 attributes of God.

17. RELAX: 10 minutes.

The first three chakras are often referred to as 'the lower triangle.' They deal with the physical needs of the body and the basic earthly needs of life - survival, creativity, and will power. They focus on elimination and reduction. It is in the lower triangle that we experience our individuality and achieve a sense of our own identity. It is in our uniqueness that we identify not only who we are, but also what we want and how to accomplish our goals.

The fourth chakra (heart) is the bridge between the two triangles, where the shift happens from ME to WE (Individual to Universal) with life experience. The balance point in the body between the flow of the upper energies of the Heavens and the lower energies of the Earth. The heart informs the earthly efforts through love and compassion, with the infinite qualities of the soul - truth, wisdom, intuition and humility. When all these are working together, it makes for a balanced, creative human being.

The upper three chakras are referred to as 'the upper triangle.' The upper three correspond to the transcendent nature of the human being - spoken truth or power of the word intuition and wisdom, and finally, humility and divinity. The chakras in the upper triangle and the aura (which combines the effects of the other seven chakras) accumulate, create, and refine the energy.

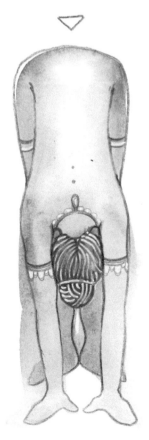

Power Kriyas

SAT KRIYA

Sat Kriya is fundamental to Kundalini Yoga and is a complete and powerful exercise in itself. Yogi Bhajan referred to it as an "entire yoga class in one posture".

How it works and what it does:
The rhythmic contraction and relaxation of the navel point creates a powerful pump to stimulate, release and circulate your Kundalini energy. It balances the prana and apana at the navel centre. The pulsing at the navel creates an internal massage which helps with digestive issues.

This movement tunes up the nervous system, improves our overall health, and even works on overcoming fears and phobias.

Sat Kriya strengthens the sexual system. By stimulating our natural energy flow it enables control of sexual phobias, and rechannels energy to creative and healing activities. It has the power to excavate deeply entrenched wounds from our early life and is often recommended for healing mental and psychological imbalances.

Yogi Bhajan proclaimed, "Sat Kriya is to purify your being. Disease, ailment, weakness, impotency, laziness, and negativity — all improper things will leave you."

If you have not taken drugs, or have cleared your system of all their effects, you may choose to practice Sat Kriya with the palms open, pressing against each other. This releases more energy, but is not generally taught in a public class, because someone may have weak nerves from drug abuse.

Caution: Practice Sat Kriya very gently if you are on your menstrual cycle or during pregnancy.

How to do it:
Sit on your heels in Rock Pose. Stretch your arms over head. Elbows straight with arms hugging the ears. Interlace all fingers except the index (Jupiter) fingers. For Sun, male energy cross your right thumb over left. For Moon, female energy cross your left thumb over right.

Bring your eyes to focus at the brow point. Begin to chant "SAT NAM" with a constant rhythm of about 8 x per 10 seconds. As you pull the navel in and up toward the spine, chant "SAT" from the Navel Point. With the sound "NAM," relax the belly. The breath regulates itself.
Start with **3 minutes** and gradually increase to **31 minutes** and relax for twice as long as your practice.

To End:
Inhale and gently squeeze the muscles of the buttocks all the way up along the spine. Hold it briefly while you concentrate on the area just above the top of the head. Exhale. Inhale. Exhale. Hold the breath out as you apply Mahabandha for 5 to 20 seconds. Relax.

SAT KRIYA WORKOUT

This kriya energizes and balances the lower triangle. It is helps with digestive and sexual ailments. Gives endurance while producing a pleasant sweat which is cleansing for your complexion. As muscles build, you will walk with increased grace and certainty. Transition smoothly from one posture to the next. Concentrate on the centres and keep neck lock in Sat Kriya. This Kriya is powerful so make time for a long savasana.

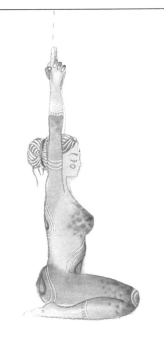

1. SAT KRIYA:
Begin chanting Sat Nam in the rhythm and style of Sat Kriya.
5 minutes. Inhale, exhale and apply mulbandh. Keep the upper body stable. Relax on back **3 minutes.**
Repeat entire sequence.
Modifications: If you unable to keep arms up, bring the mudra in front of navel with Jupiter fingers parallel to the earth.

2. CHEST STRETCH:
Interlace fingers behind your neck. Stretch elbows to the sides. Concentrate on the brow with Long Deep Breathing.
3 minutes. Inhale, hold briefly and relax.

3. SAT KRIYA:
3 minutes. Relax **2 minutes.**

4. FROG POSE:
Squat down into the Frog Pose. Keep heels lifted off ground and touching. Inhale as the buttocks up and the head goes toward the knees. Exhale as you return to the squat position, head up. The fingertips stay placed on the ground in front of the feet throughout the motion.
Repeat the frog pose **26 times.** Relax **1 minute.**

5. SAT KRIYA: 3 minutes. Relax **1 minute.**

6. FROG POSE: 10 times.
Immediately go to the next exercise.

7. SAT KRIYA: for **3 minutes.** No rest.

8. FROG POSE: 15 times. No rest.

9. SAT KRIYA: 3 minutes. No rest.

10. FROG POSE: 10 times. No rest.

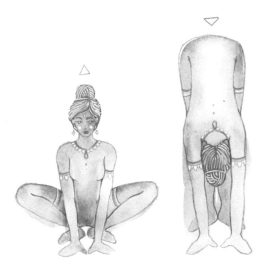

11. SAT KRIYA: 5 minutes.
To end Inhale deeply, hold with mulbandh for **30 seconds.**
Exhale completely and hold the breath out with mahabandh as long as is comfortable.
Repeat 2 more times.

12. RELAX for **15 minutes.**

DIGESTING LIFE

These exercises work on the bowel system. Normally when one is becoming sick,
the bowel movements serve as an early indicator.
It is suggested to do these exercises for 30 minutes a day for good health.

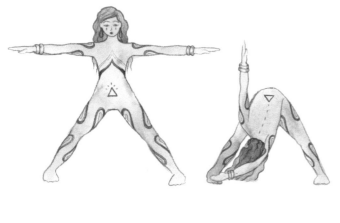

1. WINDMILL:

Stand with feet 3-4 feet apart. Bring the arms straight out parallel to ground, palms down. Bend forward from the waist, twist toward the left, bringing the right hand to the left foot and the left arm straight up. **1 minute.**

10 seconds per cycle. Switch sides for **1 minute.**

Benefits: Strengthens the abdominal, upper back, and shoulders, and stretches the hamstrings, calves, hips, lower back, and spine. Allows the heart centre to shine.
Relieves anxiety. Gives liver, kidneys, and spleen a good rinse, washing toxins out of our systems.

2. Continue the same motion but alternate sides pausing for **5 seconds** when your hand touches your foot. **3 minutes.**

3. Continue the same alternating motion, but pause for **25 seconds** as the hand touches each foot. **2 minutes.**

4. Hold position touching the foot for **2 minutes** on each side.

5. RELAX: 3 minutes.

6. STANDING SIDE BENDS:

Stand with the feet hip distance apart. Stretching the arms straight up over the head. Inhale. As you exhale arc to the left allowing your left arm to reach toward your left knee.
Right arm stretches over head toward the left. Alternate smoothly from side to side. **6 seconds** per side. **1 minute.**

Benefits: Stretches the intercostal muscles.
Stimulates the liver. Balances left and right side of the body.
Ida, Pingala. Sun, Moon. Male, Female.

7. STANDING TORSO TWIST:

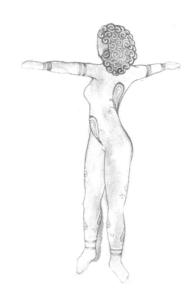

Start in the position of the previous exercise. Twist the torso and arms all the way to the left back to original position.
Then twist on around to the right and back to the centre keeping the arms in a straight line with each other.
3 seconds per complete cycle. **1 minute.**

Benefits: Keeps fascia healthy and lubricated.

8. RELAX: 10 minutes.

CHAKRA KRIYA

This set is a quick energy boost to regenerate and beautify the outer and inner environment from the root to the crown in as little as 15 minutes. It can be done as a warm up or used as a short kriya to prepare the body for a longer meditation.

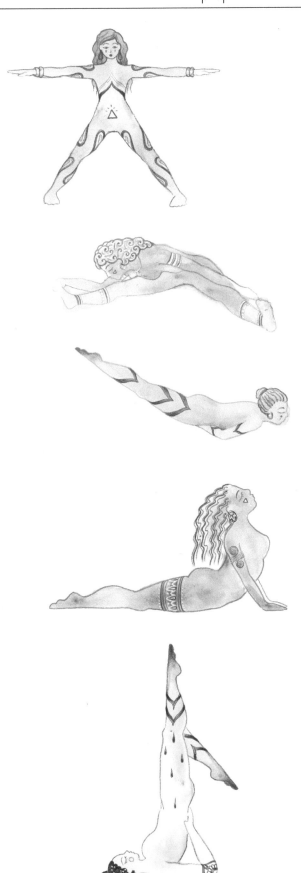

1. STANDING:

Stand with feet 3-4 feet apart. Arms straight out. Breath of Fire. **2 minutes.** Inhale slowly raising arms overhead until thumbs meet, arch back, and exhaling, slowly bend forward to touch the floor.
Benefits: Charges aura and stimulates the whole body.

2. WIDE-ANGLE SEATED FORWARD BEND:

Hold big toes of each foot. Thumb pressing the toenail. Fold toward your left knee. Breath of Fire for **2 minutes.**
To end: exhale, apply Mulbhand for as long as possible. Relax. Repeat on right side. **Benefits:** Stretches the legs. Releases groins. Stimulates lymph nodes in upper chest and pelvic area.

3. LOCUST POSE:

Make fists with the hands and place them under your hips near the groin. Heels together and the legs straight. Lift legs up as high as possible. Breath of Fire. **3 minutes.**
Modifications: Cross ankles or lift one leg at a time.
Benefits: Strengthens kidneys, adrenals, nervous system, and lower back. Moves stagnant energy in the lower 3 chakras.

4. COBRA POSE:

Concentrating at the 3rd eye, arch up into Cobra. Inhale, exhale, apply Mulbhand, holding as long as possible. Repeat for **3 minutes.** Relax **2 minutes.**
Modifications: Rest on your forearms, in sphinx pose with elbows directly under your shoulders. **Benefits:** Breath retention raises our levels of anxiety. With focus and effort we are able to release deep rooted fears. Fear is the emotion associated with the kidneys. Strengthens lower back, kidneys and spine. Invigorates our heart. Mood uplifter.

5. SHOULDER STAND:

On back, raise legs and hips perpendicular to the floor, supporting them with the hands, weight on shoulders and upper arms. Take 3 deep breaths, and on 3rd exhale apply Mulbhand, kicking buttocks rapidly with alternate heels for as long as possible. Inhale, repeat and continue for **3 minutes.**
Modifications: Stay on your back and raise legs up at 90°
Benefits: Yogi Bhajan talks about shoulder stand being the ultimate youth and beauty asana. It takes pressure off the internal organs. Massages thyroid and parathyroid for the metabolism and health of our bones.

6. RELAX: 5 - 10 minutes.

PAVAN SODHUNG KRIYA

Pavan Sodhung Kriya is an excellent liver detox as well as digestive system primer that will heal your liver and help you prevent constipation and other digestive related issues.
Working on the liver and breath retention assists in removing deep seated fears.

Make sure your body is warmed up before beginning this kriya.

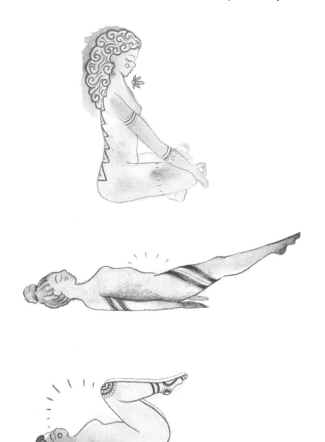

1. BREATH WARM UP:

Sit in an easy pose with your fingers in Gyan Mudra. Inhale and mentally repeat Sa Ta Na Ma. Exhale for Sa Ta Na Ma. Hold your breath out and mentally **repeat Sa Ta Na Ma 3x** while pumping your stomach. **5 minutes.**

2. LEG RAISES:

Inhale in as you raise your legs to 60° **(a) 15 seconds**
Exhale as you bring your knees in towards your chest.
Breath held out **(b) 15 seconds.**
Repeat position **(a)** as you inhale. **15 seconds** breath held in.
Lower your legs as you exhale. Remain in this position for up to **15 seconds** with your breath held out. **Repeat 8 x**
Modifications: Reduce time proportionately.
Benefits: Strengthens the navel and magnetic field; will-power opportunities and radiance.

Breath retention: More blood to your brain and heart (vasodilation). More air to enter your lungs (bronchdilitation). Calms the nervous system. Reduces your need and craving for heavy, processed and acid food. Balances digestive system. Massages the liver.

3. RELAX.

Holding the breath creates such a calm in the autonomic nervous system that the inner organs get a rest, which they otherwise never do, neither during sleep nor during the waking state.
~ Sri Yukteswar

KNOW YOUR ANGLES

The angles we make with our bodies in different postures effect the flow of energy. It is useful to know effects on the body of lifting your legs to different heights • **6°** ovaries/sex glands • **11°** everything below the navel point • **45°** navel point and kidneys • **60°** liver, spleen, gall bladder and pancreas • **70°** liver, upper stomach and gall bladder • **80°** heart, lungs, stomach **90°** our memory, control centres of the brain: pineal, pituitary glands and hypothalamus.

FEARLESS CLEANSE

Fearless cleanse kriya gives a massage to the organ body particularly to the abdomen, liver and kidneys. Energetically, the Kidneys fundamental energy is willpower and drive while the liver is responsible for a smooth flow of emotions, perspective and vision in life.

Make sure your body is warmed up before beginning this kriya.

1. COBRA POSE:

Place your hands under your shoulders. Stretch and lengthen through your lower back. Strengthen your legs with your elbows slightly bent close to your body. Long Deep Breathing. **3 minutes.** Relax **1 minute.**

Come back up into Cobra Pose. Inhale. Hold your breath in. Apply Root Lock for as long as you comfortably can. Exhale. Inhale. Continue for **1 minute.** Relax **1 minute.**

Inhale. Exhale. Apply Root lock. Continue sealing the breath out for as long as possible. Continue holding breath out for as long as you can with each breath. **3 minutes.**

Modifications: If this is too uncomfortable in your lower back, extend your hands slightly forward in front of your shoulders.

Benefits: Strengthens the arms, upper back and shoulders. Holding the breath stimulates fear in our psyche, but when we consciously hold our breath we are able to release deep emotional blockages. Prepares the body for Peacock Pose.

2. PEACOCK:

Kneel on the floor, knees wide, and sit on your heels. Lean forward and press your palms on the floor with the heels of your palms facing away from you. (Thumbs pointing out to the sides). Bend your elbows. Lean your trunk over your upper arms and lift your legs straight back as you extend the crown of your head forward.

Inhale. Exhale. Apply Root lock. Continue sealing the breath out for as long as possible. Continue holding breath out for as long as you can with each breath. Come in and out of the posture with each breath. **3 minutes.**

Modification: Raise one leg at a time at equal intervals.

Benefits: Removes toxins and detoxifies your body. Improves digestive system. Strengthens and tones your reproductive system. Reduces anxiety and stress and give calmness to the mind. Increases your focusing power of the mind. Stimulates the lymph system. A heart chakra opener. In Indian mythology, the peacock is a symbol of love and everlasting status.

3. RELAX.

KRIYA FOR VISHUDDHA CHAKRA

This short kriya directs healing energy to the neck (5th Chakra) and thyroid glands. This set uses the mantra ONG SO HUNG "Creative Consciousness I am that." The throat center represents our ability to speak up and communicate truthfully and also really listen to what is being presented to us.

1. CHEST STRETCH:

Interlace fingers behind your neck. Stretch elbows to the sides. Concentrate on the brow with **8 x** Long Deep Breaths. Begin Breath of Fire **1 minute.** Inhale. Exhale. Apply Root lock. Continue Breath of Fire **3 minutes.**

Benefits: Flushes the lymphatic system. The breath generates vitality which is the main ingredient to health and youthfulness.

2. BABY POSE:

Bring your forehead to the floor and Chant ONG SOHUNG for **3 minutes.**

Modification: Make soft fists to rest your head upon. Allow any tightness in your neck to release.

Benefits: Lower back relief. Improves digestion. Sound vibration provides physical, mental and emotional relief. Chanting is a powerful way to activate the throat chakra. Bring energy to higher glands to open our intuition and deeper perception.

3. BICYCLE POSE:

On back bend knees to your chest and begin cycling your legs in big circles as if you were on a bicycle. **2 minutes.** Reverse direction. **2 minutes.**

Benefits: Looses hips and knee joints. Massages abdominal organs and helps relieve gas. Improves overall circulation. Invigorates the whole body.

4. COW POSE:

Arch your spine down and raise the head and look up at ceiling. Long Deep Breathing. **2 minutes.**

Benefits: Eye gaze balances the hemispheres of your brain. Strengthens and tones the optic nerves and muscles of your eye. Stretches and lengthens the back torso and neck.

5. CAT/COW POSE:

Stay on your hands and knees. Arch your spine down and raise the head with the inhale. Exhale, arch the spine up and lower the head. **1 minute.**

Benefits: Increases flexibility of the neck, shoulders, and spine. Irons out tension build up in the spine. Opens and creates space through the entire neck.

6. RELAX: 5 - 10 minutes.

KRIYA FOR PRANA ABSORPTION

When the energies of prana and apana are properly mixed, the power of the Kundalini can be released. Prana is the life force we receive. Apana is the energy we give back. This set enhances the absorption and distribution of prana for a healthy body and a clear mind.

1. ROCK POSE:
Kneel and sit on heels with tops of feet on the ground to press the nerves in the center of the buttocks. Venus lock mudra on lap or fold arms across diaphragm holding opposite elbows. Gently sway from side to side. **3 minutes.**

Benefits: Improves circulation in the body. Modifies the blood flow by reducing the flow in lower portion, especially the legs and increasing blood flow to the digestive organs resulting in efficiency of the digestive system.

(It is named "Rock Pose" because it is said that its effect on the digestive system enables one to digest rocks).

You are alive by breath, you are a product of breath, and your realization is through breath. The moment you are in touch with your breath, the universe pours into you. ~ Yogi Bhajan

2. KUNDALINI LOTUS:
Bend Knees. Hold big toes with index and middle finger. Extend the legs up and out to 60°, stretching them wide apart as you straighten them. Feel the chest expand and the heart center open. **3 minutes.**

Modification: Keep the legs slightly bent to keep the spine straight. It is important not to collapse the spine.

Benefits: Brings mental and physical balance.
Channels energy from the root and second chakra into the navel which is the gateway to the heart center.

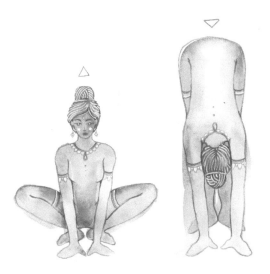

3. FROG POSE:
Squat down into the Frog Pose. Keep heels lifted off ground and touching. Inhale as the buttocks move up and the head goes toward the knees. Exhale as you return to the squat position, head up. The fingertips stay placed on the ground in front of the feet throughout the motion.

Repeat the frog pose **26 times.**

Benefits: Energises and activates the first, second, and third chakras and moves the energy up to the higher centers.

4. RELAX: 5 - 10 minutes.

The mind should dance with the body, the whole universe is your stage, the soul your choreographer.

Try to feel that whatever you are doing is the most beautiful thing, the prettiest dance, because you dance with the whole universe.

Don't resent anything. Forgive everything.
Express your essence. Let your heart guide you,
free of all limitation, regimentation, and fear.

THE MIND AND MEDITATION

*"We have the fastest and the most wonderful power—our own mind. It can take us to God.
It can take us to ourselves. It can take us deep into our self or far out into the Universe.
When clean and open, the mind can do anything that we want."*

THE MIND is a good friend with high capacity when it is in your service. It is also a potential distracter; and can be a tyrant when you are lost in the grip of the mind. Since it needs to be in service, it is important to invest in getting to know your mind so that you can master your mind and let it work for you, brilliantly. When the mind is balanced and you are in tune with it, to guide and direct it, you will find it effortless to flow with your life. It will feel as if you "do what you are meant to do" and "meant to be". When your senses are clear and sharp, and you are awake to the processes of sensing and thinking, you notice the space around you: beauty, and danger. You will notice what is happening in your body, for instance if a food is good for you or not. This is the gift of the alert and balanced mind, in combination with clear senses.

Hence we spend considerable time in Kundalini yoga working on and with our minds. We "behold" and "befriend" our minds. and make clear the order and ranking in relation to the mind: you are in charge and the mind follows you. Then you will find that your life comes into a natural order and you cease to approach it from a place of struggle.

Yogi Bhajan speaks about the mind as "dancing with the body": **The mind should dance with the body, the whole universe is your stage, the soul your choreographer. Try to feel that whatever you're doing is the most beautiful thing, the most beautiful dance, because you dance with the whole universe. Don't listen to anything. Forgive everything, express your essence. Let your heart guide you, free from any limitation, stiffening and fear.**

With time and regular practice, the Kundalini yogi begins to experience consciously this dance between mind, body and soul. It is the role of the teacher to guide the student in this balancing and tuning process. As a teacher you will do this based on your own exploration of your mind in all its complexity and brilliance and with all its challenges.
The mind is reactive and can "fire" over 1000 thoughts per second in response to a situation. This process is much faster than we can think consciously. The mind also holds many aspects and levels of a situation concurrently.
There are three functional "mind bodies". For instance, when you meet a new situation, your negative mind will page rapidly through similar experiences in your life to give you the run down on potential risks. Your positive mind will assess the benefits and opportunities of the situation and cheer you

on to make the most of them. Your neutral mind will activate the balanced state that is beyond "good or bad". In this way you will be able to make decisions "from the middle ground", centred in what is good for you and those around you.

All impulses to the mind originate from the soul. They may then enter into the realm of thought through the use of the intellect. Intellect is a part of the mind. However, the mind is at once receiving the thought from the soul and releasing it through part of itself, the intellect. You can imagine what may happen when the mind is not clear and sharp in that instance. Multiple biases, attachments and subconscious clutter may be projected through the thought process into the emotional realm. The emotions in turn produce further thoughts and exacerbate them, like a multiple (possibly distorting) mirror.

Soon, we have the whole "carousel" phenomenon that we may sometimes experience when our minds are not balanced: thoughts go in circles; we become exhausted by the mind taking us on a ride, slaves to our desires, yet not satisfied by how we fulfil them until we manage to slow down and take charge again of this process. How does this work?
This is where the will comes in, emanating from the soul. You can use the support of your breath as your most direct connection to the infinite.

There are many kriyas and meditations that focus directly on calming, balancing and guiding the mind. Specifically for training the neutral mind so that it can function to be that "voice beyond the polarities" that stretch us continuously.

Something like setting a clear intention at the beginning of practice is also a good way of taking charge and guiding the mind to be in service. Yoga teacher Donna Farhi describes this as follows:
Our intention needs to be sincere. We may have a desire to release pent-up anxiety and to feel more relaxed in life. Maybe we've got back pain and we'd like to heal our injury, or we've become overweight and we have made a commitment to become healthier. We might want to clear our mind so we can move into the day without yesterday's baggage weighing us down. I cannot stress enough the importance of setting an intention at the beginning of practice, for this sets the stage for all that will follow.
When we set the table for honored guests, we remove clutter, arrange the mats, plates, cutlery and glasses in a way that is

pleasant to the eye and when our friends arrive, a mood has been created that influences what may happen in our coming together. How different our friends would feel if they sat down to a table covered in crumbs, old papers strewn in disarray and a heap of knives and forks! This too, sets a stage for the tone of our gathering. So when we begin to practice with a conscious intention, we set the stage for what is to come.

There is always more to learn and the idea is to approach this gradually, especially when you are stepping into teaching. Take your time and get to know your own mind through practice.

MEDITATION

With the mind firing away at 1000 thoughts per second, meditation is the art and practice of "stilling the mind". The mind will keep on moving, will keep on thinking, but you will sit at a still centre without being carried away by this continuous flow of thoughts and the subsequent waves of emotions. In the beginning of this practice the mind can be trained by focusing on the breath. Give the mind something to do, like watching the in and outflow of air through the nostrils and into the lungs, then back out. Watch the pause between the breaths. We work with mantra, repetition of sound to calm the mind. The mind likes to be occupied and to have a task. In meditation we reach for a taste of that which lies beyond the realm of thinking and feeling.

Yogi Bhajan says: "In prayer the (hu)man(s) talk to God. In meditation, God talks to (the hu)man(s)."
In our meditation practice, we connect to the vast infinity that lies beyond what can be seen and grasped in the manifest world. Listen for the deep silence between the sounds, the place from which the sound arises. Sense into emptiness beyond feelings. Meditation is the practice of connecting with that place of "no-thought". It is a connection with your soul, the place of intimate connection with God. The realisation here is that I belong. I am included. I am part of infinity.

One key to meditation is regular practice. It does not matter how often you find yourself caught up in mental chatter when trying to meditate. What matters is that you notice the wanderings of the mind, catch the distractions and guide the mind back to the noticing space. Noticing the breath. Observing a thought arise and dissolve again. Watching emotions, triggered by the thought. Noticing how they come and go. We come to realise their impermanence and become less attached to them. We realise there is something beyond what we consider real, that is in fact more real.

Somehow our day goes well, despite obstacles and challenges. We manage to meet all that comes our way from a more centered place. You may find, with regular practice that your reaction and habitual patterns begin to shift and change. You are less likely to react to things that triggered you in the past. You find that little pause, just before you jump into reaction and you become able to respond instead.

In this process, our lives become "ensouled" once more, lived from a place of connection with self and with all that is. That is why, in Kundalini Yoga, much of our practice on the mat is in preparation for meditation. We prepare with asanas, pranayam and other tools for the experience of union with the divine and seek peace in our own inner infinity. We then take this experience back to the outer world, to practice our yoga "off the mat", offering attention, kindness and compassion to those around us. We know when to swing into action and when to be receptive. We become more intuitive, in a precise manner.

We do not need to have a "great experience" or a "revelation" in meditation. Seeking a thrill or chasing the profound might be based on a misunderstanding of what meditation entails. The subtle magic is enveloped in the ordinary nature of practice, each time, each moment, in the daily commitment to doing it. Once you engage, for instance, in a 40 or 90 or 120 day meditation, you may find that your experience and your moods on the mat change like seasons or seem like the weather. One day you absolutely love it, another day you dread it, yet another you feel bored and annoyed only to be inspired again the following day. It can be a roller coaster journey initially, or you may find yourself stop-starting numerous times. No worries, return and keep going. At the core, meditation is to your mind what sweeping your floors is to your cleanliness at home, or brushing your teeth to your mouth hygiene. A fellow practitioner put it like this: "Meditation is the mental floss for mental dross..."
You clean out your mental, physical and emotional "home" through practice so that the divine guest can enter. It does not matter whether this guest arrives, on time, or at all in that particular session. The readiness and dedication, the preparation and presence, the invitation into a clear, clean, empty inner space is offered again and again. You keep tending to that purified and calm mind. The rest will arrive in its own unique form that your personal meditation path will take you on.

It is a journey. Try it, stay with it, commit. Fail, falter, and come back. Always come back once you remember. You may walk away and back a thousand times. You may feel that you have fallen asleep and need to wake up again. It is all part of the process, so expect the tests to come to you. You may have started out very enthusiastically and then find yourself without an inch of energy to practice. Show up anyway and do what you can. As long as you do that, you will see that the riches of meditation are gradually revealed to you, like a slow unpeeling of layers and layers. You will find: more of you. And you will love that you, a little more each day.

THE LONGEVITY KRIYA

This kriya brings renewal and longevity. It's said to change the molecular structure of your body and mind. If there is anything in your life that you feel needs to be rejuvenated do this kriya for 40 days. Yogi Bhajan said you can "rebuild the molecular structure and align yourself with the angular rays of the sun."

PART 1: In Easy Pose, raise your right arm up to 60° in front of you and bring your left arm in a 60° angle pointing downward behind you. The two arms should form a straight 60° line. Keep the elbows stretched and the Jupiter (index) finger of each hand extended with the thumb locking down the other fingers. The palm of the right hand mudra is downward and the palm of the left hand mudra is upward. The closed eyes are focused at the centre of the chin, the Moon Centre. Breathe slowly and deeply. Sit with a straight spine and let your body go through its changes.
3 Minutes. Move straight into part 2.

PART 2: Keeping the same arm position, extend the Mercury (baby) finger with the Jupiter finger. Lock the other fingers down with the thumb. Stretch the arms straight and keep the focus at the centre of the chin. Breathe slowly and deeply.
3 Minutes. Continue to part 3.

PART 3: Still maintaining the arm position, extend all the fingers. Tighten all the muscles of the body and stretch the arms. Eyes remain focused at the centre of the chin. Continue to breathe slowly and deeply. **3 Minutes.**
Inhale, hold the breath for 10 seconds, stretch and tighten all the muscles of the body. Exhale and repeat this sequence two more times. Relax.

Benefits: The moon point helps with balancing your emotional state. The index finger promotes Jupiter energy; expansive, prosperous, generous, healing energy. The little Mercury finger promotes circulation of the energy. Part 3 balances the five tattvas in us: earth, water, fire, air, ether, as well as bringing the five vayus, the pranas into balance. Brings the nervous system into an upgrade. Let your body shake. Lock this into your body.

This meditation must NOT be done for more than 9 minutes.

Keep the path of meditation to the point that you cleanse yourself, so that you can come out of the wounds.
~ Yogi Bhajan

CHII-A KRIYA: SURROUND YOURSELF WITH PROTECTION

Yogi Bhajan said "When there comes a moment in your life when nothing works, if all shelter and hope is gone, when the enemies overcome and friends have left, do this meditation. The sound current has an Infinite power. It is the only power that is given to the human to excel. Guru Nanak explained it, 'Through the mouth you utter a sound current, to which God listens with love'."

Sit in Easy Pose. Touch the tip of the thumb to the tip of the Jupiter finger (index finger). The other fingers are relaxed. With your hands in gyan mudra, close your eyes, and move your arms in the following sequence.
Chant using the tip of your tongue.

Chant **HAR and** Stretch your arms out to the sides, angled like a "V", palms facing forward. Gently pulse your navel in slightly, gathering the energy here, the source of all things.
As you chant **HARAY** bring your elbows to the base of your ribs with your palms down. Your forearms are parallel to the earth out in front of your body.
Chant **HAREE** and bring your hands up by your shoulders, palms facing out as if you are taking a double oath.
Repeat sequence with **WAH,** stretch your arms out to the sides again. **HAY,** Bring your arms directly to the front, palms down. **GURU** hands up near your shoulders.
Continue for **11 minutes** with your eyes focused at your 3rd eye point.

To end: Inhale, hold the breath **15-20 seconds,** keep your arms in double oath position and squeeze your rib cage as you stretch your spine upward. Exhale. Repeat this sequence two more times.

Benefits: Movement of the arms provide a gentle workout for the lymphatic, immune and circulatory system.
Yogi Bhajan said "The mantra Har, Haray, Haree, Wahe Guru has six sounds. Don't take it only as a mantra, these six (Chii-a) sounds are unchangeable sounds. What surrounds you is six: the four directions, up, and down. Meditate on these six in this way and they will cover you."
Har - source of all. Haray - Flowing through. Haree - Flower of the bloom. Wahe Guru - Calling on great consciousness to bring ecstasy into our lives.

LONG EK ONG KAR

Also known as Morning Call, Long Chant, and the Adi Shakti Mantra, is said to open all the chakras, charge the solar centres, connect the soul to the Universal Soul, and liberate us from the cycle of karma. If you truly want to feel alive, this is one of the best practices to start your day with. The Kundalini energy opens up the subtle energy channels in our bodies allowing the life force to flow and expand within us.

EASY POSE: Focus on the brow point.

MUDRA: Place the hands in Gyan Mudra.

MANTRA:
Ek Ong Kar Sat Nam Siri Wahe Guru.
There is one creative force whose true essence is beyond description.

BREATH: This mantra is chanted on two and a half breaths - one complete breath for each of the first two lines, and the final line being done on half a breath.

Take a deep breath and chant "Ek Ong Kar." The "Ek" is very short; the "Ong" and "Kar" are long and equal in length. Take a second deep breath and chant "Sat Nam Siri." The "Sat" is very short, like "Ek." The "Nam" is very long (like "Ong" and "Kar") with "Siri" just escaping your tongue with the last bit of breath. Take the short half breath and chant "Wa-Hey Guru." "Wahe" and "Gu" are very short; "ru" is slightly longer.

TIME: 7, 11, 31, or 62 minutes or 2 ½ hours.

TO END: Inhale deeply, hold the breath, and focus at the Brow Point for several seconds, then exhale and relax.

TIPS FOR PRACTICE:

**It is best to use a light blanket or shawl to keep the spine free from drafts.

**Make sure you don't let the tone drop, and if it does, bring it back up.

**You can simply chant the mantra correctly to achieve great effect by the appropriate application of body locks and the energy will move through the chakras regardless of any visualisation. It's easy to get too hung up in our heads during meditation rather than just letting the mantra and breath technique work. An additional technique is visually weaving the mantra through the chakras whilst chanting as described by YB:

"Chant from the navel in a 2 1/2 breath cycle. Ek Ong Kaar – Sat Naam Siree – Wah-hay Guroo. Each sound vibrates and integrates a different chakra within the aura. Ek is very short, as when we split the atom, releasing a humongous amount of energy from the first chakra. Ong is vibrated from the second chakra, resonating through the nostrils to experience the conch of the third eye. Kaar is vibrated from the navel. Take another deep inhale and chant Sat Naam Siree. Sat is short, coming abruptly from the navel, pulling up the diaphragm. Naam is very long and resonates through the heart. Siree is the greatest of all powers, the Shakti, and is chanted with the last bit of breath. It is pulled from the navel and up through the neck lock. Then take a short breath and chant Wah-hay Guroo. Wah-hay and Guroo are released through the top of the head. Through this meditation you will master the power of prana, Pavan Siddhi, until the breath of life becomes your own. It will give you the power of Vac Siddhi, the power of speech. What you say with the breath shall happen. It is hard labor. Do this Jaap, repeating it again and again until you reach 1/10th of the day: 2 1/2 hours. Your faces will be bright and beautiful and you will settle the accounts of everyone you know." ~ Yogi Bhajan, A Year with the Master, July 20, 2000.

MASTERS TOUCH

"The Master's Touch is like a Philosopher's Stone, any matter which touches that stone becomes gold. In the Age of Aquarius, the message is, 'Take me where I can get experience', that is the difference. Experience means work, experience is not talking, it is practice. I am grateful to that man of God who touched me and put me through it."

EASY POSE:
Eyes are 1/10 open, focused at the tip of the nose.

MAHA GYAN MUDRA:
Place the pad of the right index finger (Jupiter finger) on the pad of the left index finger, so that the finger prints are lightly touching to form an approximate 45 degree angle with the index fingers pointing upwards. Right palm faces out from the body, the left palm faces towards the body. Other fingers are curled into the palms, with the thumb over. Hold the mudra lightly in front of the heart centre, elbows resting along your rib cage with shoulders relaxed.

MANTRA:
Aad Sach, Jugaad Sach, Hai Bhee Sach, Naanak Hosee Bhee Sach - You were true in the beginning, You will be true in the future, You are even true now. You shall always be true.

Chant the mantra aloud, in a monotone. The 'ch' of 'Such' sound is emphasized, but not extended. Pull the navel point in on each Such. As you chant aloud, listen to the mantra with your inner ear. **Breath:** Take a long deep breath between each round of the mantra.

TIME: Start with **11 minutes** and build up to **2 1/2 hrs.**
To end: Inhale, hold the breath. Exhale, relax the mudra and the breath. Remain in Easy Pose, hands resting on knees in Gyan Mudra for **2 minutes.**

The Ad Such is a code that really teaches us the essence of what is unconditional love. If you understand it you know unconditional love. Unconditional love first starts with yourself. You cannot love another without yourself. When you have a good day it doesn't mean that you have arrived where you want to be. When you have a bad day it doesn't mean that you are a failure. When you do something wrong it doesn't mean that you are a bad person. You are you and that goes way deeper than your daily actions.
Always strive to hold the essence of the Ad Such mantra in mind in all your daily interactions.

"The mudra allows the Infinite energy to come through. Chanting the mantra stimulates the upper palate with the tip of the tongue, tuning the thalamus and hypothalamus. Focusing on the tip of the nose causes the frontal lobe, which controls the personality, to become like lead. At one point the pain can become so unbearable, you cannot stand it. Then it 'breaks,' and you have found what you are looking for, and that is forever. Nobody can take it away. To grow roots, you must open yourself up." Yogi Bhajan 13 July 2000.

SODARSHAN CHAKRA KRIYA

"Of all the 20 types of yoga, including Kundalini Yoga, this is the highest Kriya.
It cuts through all darkness.
It will give you a new start. It cuts through all barriers of accumulated neurosis and karma.
This Kriya never fails. It can give you all the inner happiness and bring one to a state of ecstasy in life."

Sodarshan Chakra Kriya was an ancient Brahmin purification technique. It was handed down from evolved cultures which predate history as we know it.

Each of us has accumulated emotional and karmic debris which blocks our capacity to be the best version of ourselves. According to the tantra shastras* this meditation will clear the painful patterns of the past and by doing so bring out what's best in us. This meditation has considerable powers to stabilise the mind, bring out the talents we were born to use, and help move beyond learnt patterns which block our ability to fulfilment and success.

Sodarshan Chakra Kriya and Teaching.

This meditation balances the Teacher aspect of the mind. We act as a human being not just a human doing. If the Teacher aspect is too strong, we risk a spiritual ego, which becomes too attached to the ability to detach and to be "above" normal struggles. When the Teacher aspect is too weak, we can misuse our teaching position for personal advantage. When balanced, the Teacher uses intuition to know directly what is real and what is a diversion. The response is from the Neutral Mind beyond the positives and negatives.

As you practice this meditation you may experience some residual emotions, the shadow past pain that you are processing, being resolved. Remain the impartial observer to these emotions without identifying with them.
See them and then let go.

"The tragedy of life is when the subconscious releases garbage into the conscious mind. This kriya invokes the Kundalini to give you the necessary vitality and intuition to combat the negative effects of the subconscious mind. There is no time, no place, no space, and no condition attached to this mantra. Each garbage point has its own time to clear. If you are going to clean your own garbage, you must estimate and clean it as fast as you can, or as slow as you want." Yogi Bhajan.

*Tantra shastra is a secret and most powerful science in the Indian occult tradition. It is a science which Indians have practised for centuries. Tantra shastra as a whole is the system which deals with the techniques, mediums and applications concerning the individual power and knowledge which is said to be at the depth of human consciousness.

EASY POSE: Light Neck Lock.

EYES: Tip of the nose. (Not to be done with eyes closed).

BREATH AND MANTRA:

Block the RIGHT nostril. Inhale slowly and deep through the LEFT nostril.

Mentally chant the mantra **Wha-Hay Gu-Roo 16 times.**
Pull the navel in 1/3 of the way on Wha, 2/3 further on Hay, and all the way in on Guroo.

After the **16 repetitions,** unblock the RIGHT nostril.
Close the LEFT nostril.
Exhale smoothly through the RIGHT nostril.
Repeat this breath sequence, mentally reciting the mantra and pulsing at the navel center.

TIME: 11 - 31 minutes. Master practitioners may extend this practice to **62 minutes,** then to **2-1/2 hours a day.**

To end: Inhale, hold the breath 5-10 seconds, exhale. Stretch arms up and shake your body. **1 minute** spread the energy.

RELAX: for **3-5 minutes.**

HEALING MEDITATION - SIRI GAITRI MANTRA

Pray for healing energy for our family, friends, and ourselves. "For healing at a distance, this is the mantra. It cuts across time and space so you can send healing energy to someone thousands of miles away as easily as you can send it to someone across the room." Yogi Bhajan said that this mantra is one of the most powerful healing mantras. The power of this mantra comes from its ability to connect earth and ether.

EASY POSE: Your upper arms resting against your ribs, slightly in from the sides. Your palms are flat, facing upward and pointed out from your body at a 45° angle.

MUDRA: The fingers are together with the thumbs stretched out towards the side away from the fingers. Stretch the thumb away from the fingers. The stretch in the webbing keeps the hands flat and helps maintain a stretch at the wrist. It is this stretch that helps balance the brain. When the thumb is not stretched, the wrist relaxes, the hands move upward and the mudra and its effects are compromised.
When the mudra is accurately done, you will feel energy or a pull in the centre of the palms. This creates the power to heal with your hands.

EYES: Your eyes are focused at the tip of your nose.

MANTRA: Ra Ma Da Sa, Sa Say So Hung – Sun, Moon, Earth, Infinity, I am that infinity that I belong to and contain.
Breath: Inhale and chant the complete mantra on the exhalation. Pull your navel point in as you chant the first Sa and the Hung. As you chant this mantra you complete a cycle of energy and go through the circuit of chakras. It brings balance into the core of our energetic body and floods it with new energy.

TIME: Continue chanting for **11 to 31 minutes.**

To end: Inhale deeply and hold the breath, as you offer a healing prayer. Visualize the person you wish to heal as being totally healthy, radiant, and strong. See the person completely engulfed in a healing white light and completely healed. Then exhale and inhale deeply again, hold the breath and offer the same prayer again. Exhale.
To complete, inhale deeply, stretch your arms up high and vigorously shake out your hands and fingers for several seconds. Keep the arms up and hands shaking as you exhale. Repeat two more times and relax.

As you chant the mantra you can visualize it moving up through the 7 chakras and the auric field.

RA: Root chakra
MA: Sacral chakra
DA: Navel chakra
SA: Heart chakra
SA: Throat chakra
SAY: Third Eye chakra
SO: Crown chakra
HUNG: The energy moves out the crown and down through the auric field to the root once again.

TERSHULA KRIYA

Tershula Kriya is a deep meditation that activates self-healing for familial issues and parental relationships (especially the paternal relationship). It balances the nervous system and resolves personality issues. It purifies the body and develops a focused, effective mental projection that gives you the ability to heal at a distance, through your touch or through your projection.

EASY POSE:

MUDRA: Tuck the elbows next to the ribs, forearms angling up to bring the hands (palms face up) in front of the heart. The right fingers rest on the left fingers at a 75° angle with the thumbs stretched away from the hands. The arms should form a straight line from the fingertips to the elbows.

EYES: Keep eyes closed looking straight ahead.

MANTRA: Har Har Waheguru.
Translation: The Creator is bliss, Great is the Guru.

BREATH: Inhale and exhale through the nostrils only.
Inhale, draw in the navel and then lock the breath in the body. Mentally recite the mantra as you visualise your hands surrounded by white light until you need to exhale.
As you exhale visualise lightning bolts projecting from your fingertips at an upward angle.
Exhale completely and hold the breath out, engage your root lock and mentally chant the mantra for as long as you can.
Inhale deeply and then repeat the complete breath cycle with silent mantra and the visualisations.

TIME: Start with **11 minutes** and gradually develop up to **31** or **62 minutes.**

*This meditation should be practiced in a cool spot or at night since it directly stimulates the Kundalini and generates a great deal of heat in the body.

*This meditation balances the three gunas - the three qualities that permeate all creation: rajas (activity), tamas (inertia) and sattva (transcendence). There is no physical entity without all these three dimensions. Not a single atom is free of these three dimensions of a certain static nature, of energy, and of vibrance. If these three elements are not there, you cannot hold anything together – it will break up. If it is just sattva, you won't remain here for a moment – you will be gone. If it is just rajas, it's not going to work. If it's just tamas, you will be asleep all the time. So, these three qualities are present in everything. It is just a question of to what extent you mix these things.

*It brings the three nervous systems together. The nervous system consists of three parts: Central Nervous System (sensation & motor control), Peripheral Nervous System (connects nerves to organs and limbs) and Autonomic Nervous System (emergency response:
Sympathetic- "gas pedal" & Parasympathetic- "break pedal").

Without a discipline you can never be a disciple, and without a discipline you cannot be a master, and without a discipline you cannot deliver. And without a discipline you will never know the exalted self. ~ Yogi Bhajan

SEVEN WAVE SAT NAM

Bij mantras such as Sat Naam are sounds which can totally rearrange habit patterns and open
the mind to new experiences. Yogi Bhajan refers to this meditation as the Law of Tides.
If you build this meditation to at least 31 minutes per day, the mind will be cleansed like ocean waves,
washing the sandy beach.

EASY POSE:

MUDRA: Prayer Pose. Bring the hands to the heart centre
and press the thumb knuckle into the sternum. You will find
an indentation in the upper centre of the chest. Create a firm
pressure to connect the meridians of the head and heart

BREATH AND MANTRA: Inhale deeply and chant "Saaaaaat,"
– then a very short "Nam". Vibrating Sat in six waves, and let
Naam be the seventh. On each wave of sound, thread the
sound through each chakra. Begin at the base of the spine
(rectum); move to the sex organs on the second wave; then
circulate the sound at the navel on the third; the fourth
resounds at the heart. Now move upward to the throat on
the fifth wave; the sixth resonates between the eyebrows
(third eye); then let the energy and sound radiate from the
Seventh Chakra at the top of the head through the aura, unto
Infinity. Feel yourself as the instrument of the Divine.

EYES: Focus at the Brow Point.

TIME: Continue for 11 – 31 minutes.

Yogi Bhajan Lecture Excerpts on the 7 Wave Sat Nam
Meditation from 6/14/79

"Let us purify ourselves with truth, these are vibrations. The
words I can tell you: Sat Nam. Sat represents truth; Nam
represent personified. It means the spirit of that creative God,
the cosmos, stands personified through these vibrations. It
is not a big thing. But to chant it is not a muttering. It is an
electro-physical process through which this energy is made to
circulate. That is the key, there is no big thing about it."

"You have seen the law of tides. The tide takes six coils, on
the seventh coil it goes up and then it strikes and cleanses the
shore, and goes back. This is the law of tides. If the vibrations
can be created by the bij mantra, it will cleanse the body of
negativity and the remainder will be positivity and that is a
divine light. Do it as your breath permits it, honestly, and let us
all follow."

*Prayer is when the mind is one-pointed and man talks to Infinity.
Meditation is when the mind becomes totally clean and receptive,
and Infinity talks to the man. ~ Yogi Bhajan*

Sing your heart out

This is the gift, this is sound current.
It's a permutation and combination of
sounds, which create waves to reach
Infinity, and the Infinite brings infinite
knowledge. ~ Yogi Bhajan

SOUND AND MANTRA

"Naad" is the essence of all sound – the vibrational harmony through which the Infinite can be experienced. "Naad Yoga" is the science of Naad based on the experience of how sound vibrations affect the body, mind, and spirit through the movement of the tongue, the mouth, and changes in the chemicals in the brain.

The human body works like an instrument. We have strings which vibrate into the 72000 Nadis, the subtle energy channels in the body. Sound is energy with manifestation powers which is why our words matter so much. They are very powerful in what we manifest in our lives. Even our thoughts vibrate sound at subtle levels and begin to manifest what we think. In kundalini yoga we work with sound in subtle and overt ways through meditation, recitation and mantra. In this way you have the opportunity to experience consciously the power of sound as a teacher. This is known as the Shabd Guru (shabd = sound and guru = teacher, transformative knowledge moving from lower to higher consciousness). The underlying meaning of shabd is to "cut away the ego which obstructs the truth", to clear a pathway beyond thoughts, feelings and attachments in the material world.

You will also have experienced us chanting "sat nam" in kundalini yoga. Sat is the "true reality" and Nam is your "being-ness", your creative identity, in the sense of being part of creation. The ten Sikh Gurus were yogis who could access the power of sound in ways that guided them to higher consciousness. They then scripted "maps" to this experience of the Infinite by giving us instruction on the Shabd Guru, the transformative power of sound. This happens in the form of Jappa. Jappa is the practice of chanting and reciting the essential sound currents, manifest in the guru's sharing of directive patterns of thought that counters the habitual patterns of the ego. You can use the techniques of the Shabd Guru to elevate yourself, because this is a science of sound that is very effective, almost like a "spiritual DNA" helping you to stimulate the brain to evolve into higher consciousness. It will get into your nervous system and begin to permeate every cell of your body. You need not know the meaning of the words, just copying them the best you can, with accurate breath and sound. Eventually you may find yourself in a jappa jap – repeating the sounds internally without chanting aloud. There is still a lot we are learning about this quantum technology of sound and rhythm. It is based on the notion of the Naad as the "essence of sound", a kind of "Ur-Sound". We live in an endless ocean of energy that vibrates. The entire universe, all around us, all matter and transient subtle patterns are made of sound. We can work with these sound waves at higher and lower frequencies. So when the brain seeks out sensations and our mind produces its endless internal chatter, we work through reciting specific sounds so that we can access new resources, balance and achieve a deeper understanding of ourselves.

For this journey to higher consciousness to unfold we use the power of mantra in kundalini yoga. Man = mind and Tra = wave / projection. Working with mantra is a way to consciously and intentionally work with our minds. We do this to achieve the exact projection and connection we desire in our quest for a life in union with the divine in us. Mantra is a deliberate sound that activates the naad meridian points in the roof of the mouth. The upper palate contains 84 meridian points which are stimulated by the movement of the tongue during the recitation of a mantra. We work with repetition and rhythm here in ways that stimulate the major glands, the pituitary and pineal glands, and through activation of the hypothalamus in the brain. Like typing on a computer keyboard these messages are then transmitted into instructions that regulate the chemical balance in our body. The endocrine system, the metabolism and the immune system are strengthened and adjusted to function well and maintain balance.

We have many mantras in kundalini yoga that invoke positive power, prosperity, peace of mind, breaking through inner blocks, and clearing of pathways. By chanting we produce intentional vibrational patterns that creates the desired effects. This has been studied by yogis for thousands of years to discover the most effective patterns, also known as the Science of Naad Yoga. Your personality and your power of projection then become linked directly to your authentic self, and your actions will feel strong, true and accurate to others. There are different techniques here. Scientifically, there is still a lot more to discover about the concrete impact of mantra on the brain, the glandular system and how it works in turn on the entire body through the timing and synchronisation of the tongue and breath with repetition of particular sounds.

For instance, Laya Yoga also uses the power of rhythmic, repetitive sound to awaken the chakras and transform our awareness. When you chant a Laya Yoga mantra, you can literally feel the energy rising in the spine and transmitting the vibrational pattern throughout the entire body, with the intention to awaken your intuition and heighten your perception. This happens in direct relationship with the breath and the regulated inflow of prana. Mind that this, in turn, is directly linked to the words you speak in your life. Your words become the pavan guru, the expression of higher consciousness through the air element, your breath and expression. All kundalini mantras help us to achieve eventually a state of mind in which we can access the anahat – the "infinite unstruck sound". This is when our inner vibrations are in unison with the authentic divine vibrations of self. We then manage to be in the world as our best selves, content and able to offer our contribution to others, meeting our destiny with grace.

YOGI BHAJAN:

Naad means "the essence of all sounds." All languages contain sounds, which relate to one or more of the five elements of air, fire, water, earth, and ether. Gurbani is a perfect combination and permutation of sounds relating to all the five elements in complete balance.

There are eighty-four meridian points on the upper palate of a human's mouth. One can feel that upper palate with the tongue and experience its different surfaces. There are two rows of meridian points on the upper palate and on the gum behind the upper teeth.

The tongue stimulates those meridian points, and they in turn stimulate the hypothalamus which makes the pineal gland radiate. When the pineal gland radiates, it creates an impulsation in the pituitary gland. When the pituitary gland gives impulsation, the entire glandular system secretes, and a human being obtains bliss. This is the science.

When you read and recite Gurbani, it stimulates your hypothalamus. It is totally different than any scriptures because Gurbani is made in a scientific way. One who knows the Naad knows the Aad, the primal creativity. One who knows the Aad is Parameshwar, the Supreme God.

The whole language of Gurbani has the power to make a person divine, just in its recitation, if done correctly. One need not be concerned with the meaning for a change in consciousness. Read Gurbani in the way Guru says it, and understand it, and you will be in such ecstasy you will not believe it!

Concentration on the construction of the word and the sound is the proper way to recite Gurbani. As you are creating the sound, the meaning will automatically come to you, now or later. It is just a matter of time and space. You must listen to your own construction of the Gurbani. This is the technical way in Naad Yoga.

It is a scientific and direct way to unite the finite with the Infinite Consciousness. The hypothalamus will get the same tingling. The impulsation of the pituitary will function the same way and get the other glands to secrete also in the same way as it was in the body of Guru Nanak.

Shabad brings inner balance. The shabad has the power to control you and your mind, otherwise there is no way you or your mind can be controlled. When controlled, our minds can create great things, because the power of the mind is also very infinite. When disciplined, it can change the vibrations and the magnetic psyche of the Earth. Shabad is a part of the power of God, and when the shabad merges in you, you become God.

KUNDALINI YOGA MANTRAS

A central aspect in Kundalini Yoga is the conscious use of ancient mantras. These sounds create energy vibrations that can replace negative energy with positive ones. Sound travels five times more efficiently through water than through air, and as the human body is comprised of more than 70% water, it is therefore an excellent conductor for both sound and vibration. Explore the sensations and experiences caused by the impact of chanting. Pronunciation comes with repetition and understanding the meaning of the words adds another depth to chanting.

AAD SUCH, JUGAAD SUCH, HAI BHEE SUCH, NANAK HOSEE BHEE SUCH

True in the Primal Beginning. True throughout the Ages. True Here and Now. Nanak says Truth shall ever be True. This mantra helps to remove blocks. Such is Truth and it is the sound of the Kundalini energy moving up the spine burning through impurities.

Suppose something you want to move and it's not moving. There is a block and it's not movable. Then chant this mantra. It's a lever. It is the biggest lever available to you as a mantra. You are not mind or body or soul but the commander of them. This is the vibration of total truth. ~ Yogi Bhajan

----

ADI SHAKTI, ADI SHAKTI, ADI SHAKTI, NAMO NAMO: I bow to the primal power
SARB SHAKTI, SARB SHAKTI, SARB SHAKTI, NAMO NAMO: I bow to the all encompassing power and energy
PRITHAM BHAGVATI, PRITHAM BHAGVATI, PRITHAM BHAGVATI, NAMO NAMO: I bow to that which god creates
KUNDALINI MATA SHAKTI, MATA SHAKTI, NAMO NAMO: Creative power of the Kundalini, the divine mother power, I bow

Adi Shakti calls on the names of the Divine Mother. The feminine creative aspects.
A powerful meditation which invokes courage and inspiration.

Everything comes from stress. If you want to get rid of this inner-grown stress, here is one solution. There's no power more than the power of the word, and when the word is formed through the body, the entire being is purified, relaxed. ~ Yogi Bhajan

----

AAP SAHAAEE HOAA, SACHAY DAA SACHAA DOAA, HAR, HAR, HAR

The Creator has become my protector, the Truest of the True has taken care of me. Har is the primal name / sound of the Creator. A reminder that we are always surrounded by the light

This mantra meditation from the Siri Guru Granth Sahib is a gift to you that will let you penetrate the unknown without fear. It will give you protection and mental balance. It is very simple and rhythmic. If you do it nobly it will be extremely helpful. It will totally eliminate enemies and block the impact of animosity forever. It can give you mental self-control. Yogi Bhajan

----

ARDAS BHAEE AMAR DAS GURU,
AMAR DAS GURU, ARDAS BHAEE,
RAM DAS GURU, RAM DAS GURU,
RAM DAS GURU, SACHEE SAHEE

The prayer has been given to Guru Amar Das. The prayer is manifested by Guru Ram Das. The miracle is complete.
Normally there is no power in the human but the power of prayer. And to do prayer, you have to put your mind and body together and then pray from the soul. Ardas Bahee is a mantra prayer. If you sing it, your mind, body and soul automatically combine and without saying what you want, the need of the life is adjusted. That is the beauty of this prayer. ~ Yogi Bhajan

EK ONG KAUR SAT GUR PRASAD, SAT GUR PRASAD EK ONG KAUR (Repeat 5 times to shift your mood)

There is one Creator of all Creation. All is a blessing of the One Creator. This realization comes through Guru's Grace. (This mantra is generally chanted out loud, but if circumstances make that impossible, it is also effective when chanted mentally.)

Ek Ong Kar, Sat Gur Prasad is the most powerful of all mantras. There is not anything equal to it, nor can anything explain it. Ek Ong Kar, Sat Gur Prasad is a pritam (Godly) mantra—the entire Siri Guru Granth Sahib is nothing but an explanation of this mantra. It is so strong that it elevates the self beyond duality and establishes the flow of the spirit. This mantra will make the mind so powerful that it will remove all obstacles. We call it the 'magic mantra' because its powerful effect happens quickly and lasts a long time. But it has to be chanted with reverence, in a place of reverence. When you meditate on this mantra, be sure that your surroundings are marked by serenity and reverence and that you practice it with reverence. You can mock any mantra you like except this one, because this mantra is known to have a backlash. Normally mantras have no backlash. When you chant them well, they give you the benefit, but if you chant them wrong, they don't have any ill effect. If they don't do any good, at least they won't hurt you. But, if you chant Ek Ong Kar, Sat Gur Prasad wrong, it can finish you. I must give you this basic warning. This mantra is not secret, but it is very sacred. So chant it with reverence, write it with reverence, and use it with reverence. Normally we chant to God before practicing this mantra. Either chant the Mul Mantra or the Mangala Charan Mantra before meditating to prepare yourself. ~ *Yogi Bhajan*

HAR: Creative Infinity.
This bij (seed) mantra represents the Infinite in it's creative form. This mantra is used for a very powerful prosperity meditation. It is also a mantra that develops will power.

Har is a Shakti Yog mantra, Har is the original God, and sometimes, if you chant just that one word, Har, with me, you will realize God in just a couple of seconds. ~ Yogi Bhajan

----

HAR HAR HAR HAR GOBINDAY, HAR HAR HAR HAR MUKHUNDAY,
HAR HAR HAR HAR UDHARAY, HAR HAR HAR HAR APARAY,
HAR HAR HAR HAR HARIANG, HAR HAR HAR HAR KARIANG,
HAR HAR HAR HAR NIRNAMAY, HAR HAR HAR HAR AKAMAY

The four repetitions of Har give power to all aspects and provide the power to break down barriers of the past.

"This meditation has the power of a tidal wave to take away every block to your prosperity." ~ Yogi Bhajan

----

SA RE SA SA, SA RE SA SA, SA RE SA SA, SA RUNG
HAR RE HAR HAR, HAR RE HAR HAR, HAR RE HAR HAR, HAR RUNG

That Infinite Totality is here, everywhere. That creativity of God is here, everywhere.
Sa is the Infinite, the Totality, God. It is the element of ether. It is the origin, the beginning, and it contains all other effects. It is subtle and beyond. Har is the creativity of the Earth. It is the dense element, the power of manifestation, the tangible, the personal. These sounds are woven together and then projected through the sound of Rung or complete Totality.
This is the base mantra of all mantras.

Adversity melts before this mantra. It gives you the capacity of effective communication so your words contain mastery and impact.
This mantra helps you conquer the wisdom of the past, present, and future.
It brings you peace and prosperity even if it wasn't in your destiny. ~ Yogi Bhajan

SADHANA

Sadhana is your gift to yourself, each day. We come to the yoga mat in the early hours of the morning, the Amrit Vela (literally "the ambrosial hours"). This is a time of increased permeability between the worlds, the tangible material realm and the divine, more ethereal realms.

The first part of Sadhana is showing up, at the hour before sunrise, or any time between 3-7am when the earth rotation and frequency is ideally suited to meditate. It is a time of connecting self to self and receiving enhanced balance, more life energy, wisdom and gifts along the spiritual path.

Yogi Bhajan gave the Aquarian Sadhana to practice in the decades before and after entry into the Aquarian Age (2011), so as to be able to cope with the changes and meet the new times. The Aquarian Age is "the age of experience", whereas the previous age, the Piscean Age, was "the age of knowledge". So this new time is less about how much knowledge you can gather or pass on, nor how much recognition and status you earn in return, but how to give yourself and others the experience needed to grow and mature, as a human being, and even as a human community. During these early morning hours the sun is at an angle of less than 60° to the earth. Nature and Life in your part of the planet slowly begin to awaken then. The veils are thin.

How does Sadhana work?

Ideally, you awaken at this early hour, do some stretches in bed, slowly open your eyes and greet the day. Take a cold shower to experience the power of ishnaan, water therapy. You can massage your body with almond oil before your shower and cover your upper thighs and crown from the water. Vigorously massage your arms, legs, chest, shoulders and face creating health in the organs and energising the entire body.

It is useful to dress in light colour and cover your head with a light cotton cloth during sadhana, enhancing the sense of protection and containment during strong meditation. Use natural material where possible.

Ready for the mat, we traditionally begin by chanting the Japji, a prayer offered by Guru Nanak who wrote it tracing his own route to higher consciousness. This prayer is a Naad, a sound current that creates an experiential pathway for the chanter. Just by being in the vibrations of this sound current, our higher self opens up to us. Chanting for 20-35 min is usually followed by some light warm ups or a short kriya to stimulate the body and prepare for meditation.

The crown of Sadhana is usually a longer meditation period. It is good to start with the Aquarian Sadhana that contains 7 mantras, to give you a full practice experience. Sadhana is extra powerful when done in a group setting where the collective consciousness and group vibrations will carry you through many moments of tiredness and adversity.

The essence of sadhana shows up in three steps: Sadhana, Aradhana and Prabhupati. Sadhana is your way of practice and finding your specific pathway of meditation in the early hours. It makes the mind clear for the day. It is not always easy and means at times you will conquer yourself and your tiredness and a thousand excuses not to get up. Eventually the subconscious mind will begin to wake us up at the relevant hour and things flow with ease as the subconscious begins to support us, acknowledging our commitment. This is when you reach Aradhana – the mind becomes more active and an ally in the efforts at clearing. If we can manage to stay with the practice we will reap the benefits of Aradhana cleaning out the subconscious to the full. We then enter the stage of Prabhupati which literally means "spouse of God". Here we are simply neutral, nothing much can faze us about the material world and its dualities. We experience harmony and unison even in the midst of challenge and crisis. The Aquarian Age will have many times that seem chaotic because of large shifts and changes. The task is to become awakened in ways that we can at once feel the pain and joy of the world around us, yet we stay stable in our compassionate stance towards this world. You will become open and attuned to the super consciousness, and with practice, you will be able to serve the world from that place. As a teacher you will also learn to create and practice your own personal daily Sadhana. This could be the Aquarian, or you may be working with a particular practice or meditation at the time, for instance choosing a relevant mantra for 40, 90, 120 or even a 1000 days. You need to work with Sadhana that works for you, staying committed. This practice is essential for you as a kundalini yoga teacher. It will guide and hold you in your integrity. It creates presence so that your teaching practice comes from a place that is authentic, powerful and real. It creates a teacher who is true to you, yet plugged into your higher consciousness.

Sadhana will change you. It can be a lifesaver and stabiliser in turbulent times. Sadhana is your personal commitment to yourself and to being a teacher. There will be those mornings when you "just don't feel like it". You need to come through and show up anyways. When you do, you will find a new capacity to change your own energy. You realise more of what

it means when Yogi B speaks of "commanding one's life": being the creator of your own life, rather than tagging along or being washed away.

Finding your own daily practice and attending a regular group Sadhana, you will give yourself strength and endurance. You will discover new capability when life gets tough and gritty. It is like setting your sail carefully and connecting to the winds in order to navigate your day with ease and grace, no matter what the day offers back to you. That is the power of Sadhana.

SADHANA MANTRAS

Sadhana is a committed prayer, which you want to do, have to do, and which is being done by you. It is self-enrichment. It is not something which is done to gain something. A personal process in which you bring out your best. ~ Yogi Bhajan

1. EK ONG KAR SAT NAM SIRI WAHE GURU (page 62)
I learned that every fear, every emotion, every physical discomfort could be channelled into Long Ek Ong Kars.
This mantra has the power to cleanse anything. It vibrates from the central channel, the Shushmana, and actively purifies and cleanses this channel and connects the entire chakra system. ~ Snatam Kaur

2. WAH YANTEE, KAR YANTEE, JAG DUT PATEE, AADAK IT WAAHAA, BRAHMAADEH TRESHA GURU, IT WAHE GURU

Great Macroself, Creative Self. All that is creative through time, All that is the Great One.
Three aspects of God: Brahma, Vishnu, Mahesh. That is Wahe Guru.
This mantra was given by the great Yogi Patanjali. It is said that over 2000 years ago Patanjali was lecturing students on prophets who would come in the iron age, the age of Kaliyug. He prophesied Guru Nanak Dev coming into the world and gave the "Wah Yantee" mantra which describes Wahe Guru. Chanting this mantra awakens the intuition and strengthens the relationship between your individual consciousness and the universal consciousness. God is in you, and God is in everyone.

Wah Yantee is the mantra of creativity and renewal. This is where the joy begins and the journey. The tunes for me are totally different every morning. Sometimes I am surprised by the energy of this Mantra because it is so creative in nature and yet so ancient.
It is the most secure creative energy that we have available to tap into. For any creative person out there, you must know the importance of being secure in your creativity and that is why I tap into this mantra every morning. ~ Snatam Kaur

3.	EK ONG KAR	One Creator, Creation
	SAT NAM	Truth is God's Name
	KARTAA PURKH	Doer of everything
	NIRBHAO	Fearless
	NIRVAIR	Revengeless
	AKAAL MOORAT	Undying
	AJOONEE	Unborn
	SAIBUNG	Self Illumined
	GUR PRASAD	It is by Guru's Grace
	JAP	Meditate!
	AAD SACH	True in the beginning
	HAIBHEE SACH	True even now
	NANAK HOSEE BHEE SACH	Nanak says Truth shall ever be.

The Mul Mantra, the words first spoken by the spiritual master Guru Nanak after enlightenment, literally translates as the "Root Mantra," or the mantra from which all other mantras in the Kundalini Yoga tradition are built. It contains the core, essential truth of creation, and its vibration is so powerful that it can change your fate and help you rewrite your destiny. Chanting this mantra helps you experience the depth and divinity of your soul. It can root out and burn away deep, longstanding pain and sorrow.

The Mul Mantra connects you to the Infinite Truth where there is no question, boundary, or lack of energy. Whatever thoughts or ideas that may mislead you will be corrected in this Mantra. This Mantra corrects you, without you knowing it because very simply you vibrate with its eternal truth and it becomes your eternal truth. All of a sudden things that were unbearable to deal with, challenges that you didn't know how to deal with, thoughts that kept coming back uninvited are brought to light. The eternal truth always comes into play and relaxes things… that's all that is needed. Then you see what is real and what is not. ~ Snatam Kaur.

4.	SAT SIRI, SIREE AKAL	True and Great One, Great Undying One,
	SIREE AKAL, MAHAA AKAAL	Great Undying One, Exalted One, Undying One
	MAHAA AKAAL, SAT NAM	Exalted One, Undying One, Truth is God's Name
	AKAAL MOORAT, WAHE GURU	Undying Form, Great is the Experience of the Divine

Yogi Bhajan called this the mantra for the Aquarian age. When we chant it we connect with the undying, eternal truth that is our true essence. It helps us to be victorious in all aspects of our life.

Sat Siri Akal is the Mantra that prepares us for death, for that moment when the Prana leaves the body and the soul answers for all vibrations, all thoughts, and all actions. The penetration of this Mantra helps us to guide our lives so that we take the right course on a day to day basis, and are in the Infinite Flow at the time of death. ~ Snatam Kaur.

5. **RAKHAY RAKHANHAAR AAP UBAARIUN**

Thou who savest, save us all and take us across.

GUR KEE PAIREE PAA-EH KAAJ SAVAARIUN

Uplifting and giving the excellence. You gave us the touch of the lotus feet of the Guru, and all our jobs are done.

HOAA AAP DAYAAL MANHO NA VISAARIUN

You have become merciful, kind and compassionate and so our mind does not forget Thee.

SAADH JANAA KAI SUNG BHAVJAL TAARIUN

In the company of the holy beings you take us from misfortune and calamities, scandals, and disrepute.

SAAKAT NINDAK DUSHT KHIN MAA-EH BIDAARIUN

Godless, slandeorus enemies, you finish them in timelessness.

TIS SAAHIB KEE TAYK NAANAK MANAI MAA-EH

That great Lord is my anchor. Nanak, keep Him firm in your mind.

JIS SIMRAT SUKH HO-EH SAGLAY DOOKH JAA-EH (x 2)

By meditating and repeating his Name, all happiness comes and all sorrows and pain go away.

These are the words of Guru Arjan, the 5th Sikh Guru. It is part of the Sikh evening prayer (Rehras), which adds spiritually charged energy to one's physical, emotional, mental and subtle bodies. It is a victory song which removes obstacles to fulfilling one's destiny. Victory is when we are able to be guided by and receive God's grace.

This is a shabd of protection against all negative forces which move against one's walk on the path of destiny, both inner and outer. It cuts like a sword through every opposing vibration, thought, word, and action." ~ Yogi Bhajan.

6. WAHE GURU, WAHE GURU, WAHE GURU, WAHE JIO

Wahe Guru: Wow! I am in ecstasy when I experience the Indescribable Wisdom.
The divine inner teacher, the dispeller of darkness is beyond description!

This mantra expresses the indescribable experience of going from darkness to light. It is a mantra of infinite ecstasy. It is the Gurmantra, which triggers the destiny. **Wahe Jio:** Great beyond description is the experience of God blessing the Soul.
This mantra helps negative and confusing vibrations to be cleared away at a soul level, so your pure truth can be recognized.

The Waheguru Mantra is where the chanting practice goes very deep into the psyche. First of all it is really long. So after you have gotten into it, enjoyed it, gotten thoroughly bored of it, then it takes hold of you. It is in this moment of boredom that if you stay with it and allow the rhythm of the words to keep beating on your consciousness that Guru Ram Das will come in and lift you into a place where the mind has no domain any longer, where it is between you and your soul and the vibratory frequency of your own consciousness. We all have complete awareness, we are all enlightened beings, and this Mantra takes us into that state.
~ Snatam Kaur

7. GURU GURU WAHE GURU, GURU RAM DAS GURU

This mantra is chanted in praise of the consciousness of Guru Ram Das invoking guidance, healing and protection. It allows us to embody his spiritual qualities of compassion, humility and respect for everyone and all paths. The first part is a Nirgun mantra (Guru Guru Wahe Guru) which projects the mind to the source of knowledge and ecstasy. The second part is a Sirgun mantra (Guru Ram Das Guru) which means the wisdom that comes as a servant of the infinite. It reconnects the experience of the finite to infinity.

It brings to the self a meditative peace. It's so vibratory even your lips, your upper palate, your tongue, your entire surroundings feel a vibratory effect. It's my personal mantra. It was given to me by Guru Ram Das in his astral self. The impossible becomes pure, simple, truthfully possible because you have the given values and you have given yourself—soul and spirit—to those given values righteously. It is then that God manifests everything. ~ Yogi Bhajan.

Finally we are ready for the healing of Guru Ram Das when we chant to him at the end of Sadhana. The sun is usually rising or the first light is coming depending on where you live and what time of year. But this sensation of the sun rising perfectly describes the feeling of this Mantra. It is the Infinite space where Guru Ram Das exists and you are right there with him. It is the time for your inner most prayers, the ones you didn't even know existed, the prayers that come from your Soul. ~ Snatam Kaur.

STAYING ON THE PATH

If you have found it in this lifetime, you are blessed. If you can stay with it, you are more than blessed. If you can share it, you bless the world and all who live in it. May this awareness stay with you as you become a powerful and potent teacher. May you continue to bless and mature yourself through the practice, so you can meet your students' needs and together we create that better world we all dream of.

If you are living in an urban environment and received a Western based education, you are likely to live in a mostly linear relationship with time. This is based on the chronological understanding of time. We live by a logic of progress and evolution that is rooted in the Cartesian-mechanical model of the world. Many students coming to yoga initially in westernised contexts approach the path from this conditioning, which means we want to see progress and results from our practice in a short space of time. We may also be expecting a linear kind of advancement where my efforts are continuously rewarded with better and better results.

In forming a relationship with the teachings, through practice, new avenues and possibilities may begin to open up in our lives. We may have an experience of great advancement initially, literally taking quantum leaps in life and consciousness. This can be the gift of the novice who comes with the openness of a 'Beginner's Mind''. As we continue on the path, we gradually get more of a sense of its inherent rhythms and seasons. Sometimes it will feel like spring, lots of new growth and a sense of promise. We may experience the delights of summertime where we can be in full strength and fire. Or find ourselves with a sense of "the leaves falling". Less energy. Practice and commitment may feel frustrating altogether and falter. A quieter period may come, with less enthusiasm and outer strength. Yet this period is no less important. Natural evolution includes time of "lying fallow", just like a field that regenerates when no crops are planted for a while. A kind of "re-wilding". When our practice is in its own "winter", it often is a time of integration, a time of letting be and staying with what we have learnt. We may experience "little deaths", lose our energy and enthusiasm, feel no inner fire.

We meet our ego in this period of winter. Death and dying teach us not to become too attached to the results we have achieved. We may have to let go of beliefs, perhaps of thinking what an advanced yogi I have become, or get lost in rage and anger that we thought we'd overcome. In this period we lose interest and are tempted to walk away from it all, giving in

to our ego's upset about not receiving the usual praise and recognition. And then, suddenly, when we to stay with the practice through all the frustration, challenges, low energy and "little ego deaths", the shift comes. The realisation of some of the subconscious clutter has surfaced and gone, we arrive in a new place. The world is fresh again. The practice is enlivening and rejuvenating. Spring has returned.

Approaching our yogic path from this more organic perspective (rather than as a sequence), can help understand that we will go through phases of growth and decay, of loss and gain, no matter how long or hard we practice. We cease to try to "get somewhere". Slowly we mature through each season and cycle, and we truly grow. As the years go by, 1, 2, 5, 10 and 20 years of practice we begin to realise the real extent of our growth and healing on this path. It reveals itself to us, slowly and in glimpses. We have a better sense that nothing is here to stay. The practice goes on and regression is possible at any time. Yoga as a living practice needs care, attention and regular connection, or it will wilt and whither, like any other relationship. Someone asked Yogi B: "Why do you practice when you are a Master?" He said: "To stay a Master." The story goes that even the morning after surgery Yogi B was practising his Sadhana, showing his extraordinary ability and commitment to stay on the path, no excuses.

The yogi's journey is with rigour and discipline, yet not in a self punishing way. It is letting go and releasing without needing to fight the ego that has its role and function in our existence on earth. It is being present to what is and honouring it rather than willing it to be what we want. It also means using our will to shape our life based on the wisdom and guidance received from our higher self. Progress here is not a result of relentless activity but of ongoing attention and care over time. Love for your body. Patience with your mind. Cutting the crap when you need to, invoking your warrior self. Extra hours of sleep. Tenderness, care and compassion for self. Then again more physicality and withstanding the pressure of time and the demands of the external world.

We see students burn out because they push too hard initially and approach the practice from a desire to show outward success and demonstrate "change". We live in a world that teaches us insecurity and competition rather than "enoughness" and collaboration. Yet any advancement on the yogic path can never make me "better than..." or "more successful than..." These are the shadow trappings of spiritual seeking. Being a yogi is neither a race nor a competition. When we manage to show up, this is a gift to us, not made by us, not even created by our effort. Yogi B called the practice "a Grace of God". If you have found it in this lifetime, you are blessed. If you can stay with it, you are more than blessed. If you can share it, you bless the world and all who live in it. May this awareness stay with you as you become a powerful and potent teacher. May you continue to bless and mature yourself through the practice, so you can meet your students' needs and together we create that better world we all dream of.

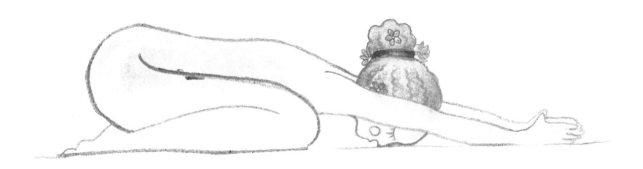

Speacial thanks to:

Yogi Bhajan for these powerful teachings

Lexi Aronson for collaborating with me on the yoga illustrations

Undine Whande on co-writing Sadhana and Mantra

CPSIA information can be obtained
at www.ICGtesting.com
Printed in the USA
LVIIW071502281220
675226LV00024B/94